Between the Said

Philosophy, Phenomenology and Hermeneutics of Values
Philosophie, Phänomenologie und Hermeneutik der Werte
Philosophie, Phénoménologie et Herméneutique des Valeurs

Book series of the Institute for Axiological Research
General Editor: Yvanka B. Raynova

Vol. 4

PETER LANG
Frankfurt am Main · Berlin · Bern · Bruxelles · New York · Oxford · Wien

Yvanka B. Raynova

Between the Said
and the Unsaid

In Conversation with Paul Ricoeur

Volume I

PETER LANG
Internationaler Verlag der Wissenschaften

Bibliographic Information published by the Deutsche Nationalbibliothek
The Deutsche Nationalbibliothek lists this publication in the Deutsche Nationalbibliografie; detailed bibliographic data is available in the internet at <http://www.d-nb.de>.

Printed with the support of the Federal Ministry of Science and Research in Vienna.

Cover illustration:
Yvanka B. Raynova and Paul Ricoeur.
© Yvanka B. Raynova

ISSN 1611-258X
ISBN 978-3-631-52452-7

© Peter Lang GmbH
Internationaler Verlag der Wissenschaften
Frankfurt am Main 2009
All rights reserved.

All parts of this publication are protected by copyright. Any utilisation outside the strict limits of the copyright law, without the permission of the publisher, is forbidden and liable to prosecution. This applies in particular to reproductions, translations, microfilming, and storage and processing in electronic retrieval systems.

www.peterlang.de

Contents

Introduction 7

1. Quo vadis? 17
2. All that "gives rise to thought" 47
3. Narrative Identity in Retrospection 107

Paul Ricoeur: A chronology with
biographical sources 147
Paul Ricoeur Primary Bibliography:
Books in French and English 153

Introduction

In his tribute to Paul Ricoeur "La parole. Donner, nommer, appeler" Jacques Derrida notes:

"Even without admitting, sincerely, a feeling of incompetence, I think never have I been so lacking the strength to tackle, by way of a study or philosophical discussion, the immense oeuvre of Paul Ricoeur. How does one limit oneself to a single place, to a single station on such a long and rich trajectory, covering so many territories, themes or problems: from ethics to psychoanalysis, from phenomenology to hermeneutics or to theology (…), through the history of philosophy and the original interpretation of so many philosophers, from Aristotle or Augustine to Kant, from Jaspers and Husserl to Heidegger or Levinas, not to mention Freud or the Anglo-Saxon philosophers that Ricoeur had the courage and lucidity (so rare in France) to read and to consider in his innovative work? It seems to me that this is a difficult task, if not impossible if I am to avoid betraying in a couple of pages the unity of a style, of an intention, of a *reflection*, but also of a passion and of a *faith, of a reflected and reflecting faith*, of an engagement which since the beginning has never broken off from a specific fidelity: fidelity to himself and to others."[1]

Indeed, how does one approach such a multiple and rich oeuvre without simplifying it or distorting its implicit

---

[1] "Sans même avouer, sincèrement, un sentiment d'incompétence, je crois que jamais la force ne m'aura autant manqué pour aborder, sous la forme d'une étude ou d'une discussion philosophique, l'œuvre immense de Paul Ricœur. Comment se limiter à l'un des lieux, à l'une des stations seulement, tout au long d'un trajectoire aussi longue, aussi riche, à travers tant de territoires, thèmes ou problèmes : de l'éthique à la psychanalyse, de la phénoménologie à l'herméneutique, voire à la théologie (…) à travers l'histoire de la philosophie, à travers l'interprétation originale de tant de philosophes, d'Aristote ou Augustin à Kant, de Jaspers et de Husserl à Heidegger ou à Levinas, sans parler de Freud, sans parler de tous les philosophes anglo-saxons que Ricœur a eu le courage et la lucidité, si rares en France, de lire, de faire lire et de prendre en compte dans son travail le plus novateur ? Cela me paraît difficile, voire impossible si l'on ne veut pas trahir, en quelques pages, l'unité d'un style et d'une intention, d'une *pensée* mais aussi d'une passion et d'une *foi, d'une foi pensée et pensante*, d'un engagement qui, depuis le début, n'a jamais cédé sur une certaine fidélité. À soi-même comme aux autres" (Jacques Derrida, "La parole. Donner, nommer, appeler," in Myriam Revault d'Allonnes, François Azouvi, ed., *Paul Ricoeur*. Paris: Editions de l'Herne, 2004, 19).

purpose? I think Ricoeur himself suggests a way when he says that his entire philosophical work is organized by some central questions or problems: "I tend to see the sequence of my books as fragments, which do not form a whole, because each one answers a different problem."[2]

The following study is divided into two parts. The first one – *Between the Said and the Unsaid* – which is published in a separate volume, presents three conversations or interviews with Paul Ricoeur that were held at different dates. They have the same purpose – to scrutinize the complex philosophical evolution of Ricoeur's thought – but they have a different focus and a different context. The first conversation took place during the World Congress of Philosophy in Moscow (August 1993), the second – during the seminar on "Memory-History-Forgetting-Forgiveness" held by Paul Ricoeur in Naples at the Instituto Italiano degli Studi Filosoofici (April 1996) and the third, also at the Instituto Italiano degli Studi Filosoofici – at his seminar "The Right to Punish", held six years later (October 2002) .

---

[2] See the first interview – "All that gives rise to thought", published here (page 20).

I should mention that I had my first opportunity to hear a lecture by Paul Ricoeur in 1988 during the World Congress of Philosophy in Brighton. This meeting was marked by two fundamental events. On the one hand, the beginning of a new dialogue between East and West which was no longer purely polemical in character, but rather was softened by the spirit of *perestroika*, quite friendly and cooperative. On the other hand however, there was the attack on philosophy, which was becoming a sensitive issue in the West, in particular through the closing of several university philosophy faculties, the shortening of philosophical programs, the dismissal of philosophy professors etc. Two years later, a new reaction against philosophy and philosophers occurred, but this time in Eastern Europe. With the collapse of Communism and the equation "Philosophy = Marxism = Communist Ideology," philosophy had not only lost its privileged status, but it was even labelled as being guilty of, and responsible for, various evils.[3] It is in this

---

[3] For more details, see my study, "Visions from the Ashes: Philosophical Life in Bulgaria from 1945 to 1992," in Barry Smith, ed., *Philosophy and Political Change in Eastern Europe* (La Salle, Illinois: The Hegeler Institute, 1993), 103-134.

context, i.e., the impeachment of philosophy and the necessity of justifying its right to exist in contemporary society and culture, that I initiated a series of interviews – with Paul Ricoeur, Richard Rorty, Enrique Dussel, and others[4] – in the hope that their "voice" would help in our fight to preserve a continued presence of philosophy in the Academy.[5] The "Appeal for Philosophy,"[6] which was proclaimed during the Moscow congress and signed by well-known personalities such as Paul Ricoeur, pursued a similar goal.

Some of the central questions which arose during our first conversation, were: Why philosophy today? In

---

[4] Ivanka Raynova, *Filosofiyata v kraya na XX vek. Razgovori s Pol Rik'or, Richard Rorti, Rikhard Viser, Enrike Dusel, i dr.* (Pleven: EA, 1995).

[5] The Institute of Philosophy in Sofia was closed and reopened twice by the Bulgarian Academy of Sciences: in 1988/89 under Jivkov's regime, with the argument that it is a nest of dissidents and enemies of Socialism, and in 1995, with the contrary argument, namely that it is a relic of Marxism and Communism.

[6] The Appeal was initiated and promoted by the Istituto Italiano degli Studi Filosofici (IISF). It was addressed to the international community and was particularly helpful to us in our situation; I translated it into Bulgarian and published it, instead of a conclusion, at the end of *Filoso-fiyata v kraya na XX vek* (148-149). An online version of the Appeal can be found in French and in Italian at the homepage of the IISF:
http://www.iisf.it/francese/appel_phil.htm and
http://www.iisf.it/appelli/app_fil.htm

what ways can philosophy help to resolve the current problems of society and humankind? At the same time, and as a phenomenologist myself, I had a deep and very particular interest in Paul Ricoeur's philosophy.[7] What worried me in my research on Ricoeur's hermeneutic phenomenology was primarily the question of how to interpret or "think together" the issues of his first works and those of his later ones, especially concerning the problems of the self and its relation to being, transcendence and language.

Consequently, the problem of the relation between philosophy and religious thought came to the forefront. The conversation in Moscow (1993) seemed to answer all of these questions, especially since Ricoeur presented, extensively and with great lucidity, the complex evolution of his thought; yet at the same time it disturbed me so profoundly that I was provoked into organizing a second interview, to discuss such contentious issues as the primary object of interpretation, the role and poten-

---

[7] I had just written the book *From Husserl to Ricoeur. The Phenomenological Approach to the Human Being* (in Bulgarian, Sofia: "Sv. Kliment Ohridksi" Sofia University Press, 1993), and had started, as general editor of a series on contemporary philosophy, a translation and publishing program of Paul Ricoeur's main works into Bulgarian, including *Le conflit des interprétations*, *Du texte à l'action*, *Soi-même comme un autre*, etc.

tiality of language, the possibility of elaborating a religious philosophy within the method of hermeneutic phenomenology, the assignments and responsibility of the philosopher, as well as Ricoeur's relation to other contemporary thinkers. The third and last interview with Paul Ricoeur took place on the 17th of October 2002 in Naples, four months before his 90th birthday. It focused on the one hand on Ricoeur's reconsideration of his intellectual biography and on the other hand on his philosophical anthropology and its relation to the questions of individual and social hermeneutics, of justice and gender difference.

For all of these questions Paul Ricoeur offers us articulated answers which, nevertheless, are not definitive. He gives us the possibility of taking different paths by investigating and rethinking those answers through his work, and perhaps more importantly, he allows us the freedom to either accept his arguments or search for better ones.

That is why in the second volume – *Hermeneutic Phenomenology between the Sacred and the Profane* – an attempt is made to reinterpret some of the central questions of Ricoeur's philosophy in the light of the three interviews. Those questions take into account some relations between different approaches or fields, like the relation between the hermeneutics of facticity and the hermeneutics of the self, between philosophy and religion or theology, between the language of the sacred and narrativity, between person and community, between will and responsibility, between rationality and violence, between values and choice, between European history and European values etc.

The aim and the methodic procedure of the reinterpretation of Ricoeur's work consists of: firstly the genetic reconstruction of each question or problem, starting with Ricoeur's early writings and working through to his last ones. Secondly, analyzing and pointing out his different methodological approaches, which often leads to tensions and contradictory answers. Thirdly, making a critical revision of these different answers in the light of our three interviews, in order to form some conclusions about Ricoeur's philosophical oeuvre as a whole.

The conversations with Paul Ricoeur and some of the studies of the second part of the book have already been published in different languages – in Bulgarian, German, English, French and Italian amongst others. I wish at this point to thank all my colleagues for their support and for enabling some of these publications – Andrzej Wiercinski, Herta Nagl-Docekal, Hans-Peter Krüger, Attilo Danese, Hans-Reiner Sepp, Michel Staudigl, Ludwig Hagedorn, Klaus Nellen. I would also like to thank Antonio Gargano for arranging my stay at the Instituto Italiano degli Studi Filosofici, as well Daniela Ianotta and Catherine Goldstein for helping with communication matters and meeting arrangements with Paul Ricoeur. But my very special thanks go to Domenico Jervolino, who not only introduced me to Paul Ricoeur in Moscow in 1993, but without whom several further meetings with Ricoeur and other important projects would not have been possible. Last but not least, I am most grateful to Rebecca White for her excellent proofreading and enormous help with the English translation of my book.

1. Quo Vadis?

Yvanka Raynova: In your self-portrait, "Ce qui me préoccupe depuis trente ans,"[8] you sketched out three stages in your evolution – reflexive philosophy, phenomenology, and hermeneutics. It seems to me, nevertheless, that, from *The Voluntary and the Involuntary* and *History and Truth* to *The Conflict of Interpretations* and *From Text to Action*, an important change has taken place in the paradigm of your thought, as well as in your approach, a sort of shift from the concrete problems of the human condition to the more abstract problems of textuality and hermeneutic methodology. But are we not in *Oneself as Another* witnesses of a sort of return to the problems that preoccupied "the young Ricoeur?"

Paul Ricoeur: I completely agree with this interpretation of my evolution. And I shall open a bracket here by saying that my readers have more right than I to interpret, because they have a certain distance from where they can see the

---

[8] See Paul Ricoeur, "Ce qui me préoccupe depuis trente ans," *Esprit* 8-9 (1986); cf. Paul Ricoeur, *Du texte à l'action* (Paris: Seuil, 1986), 25ff. [English: *From Text to Action. Essays in Hermeneutics II*. Translated by Kathleen Blamey and John B. Thompson (London: The Athlone Press, 1991), 1-20].

entirety of my philosophical work. Personally, as I say in the text you refer to, I tend to see the sequence of my books as fragments, which do not form a whole, because each one answers a different problem. Furthermore, I believe that, before speaking about the evolution of the answers, it is necessary to speak about the evolution of the questions. At the beginning it was really a question concerning the structure of human action, because Merleau-Ponty had written *The Phenomenology of Perception* and I said to myself that it was left to me to write about action. But there was the problem of symbolism, which interfered with this first very Husserlian approach, namely the description (even empirical) of will, custom, emotion, unconscious, birth and death. Thus the turning point was certainly the introduction of symbolism as an approach to the problem of evil. This was a very localized problem: What is this, the bad will? I passed from this problem to the next, by a sort of crisis. The crisis was due mainly to the encounter with psychoanalysis, because everything that I had said on bad will was bound to a very specific tradition of our culture, the tradition of Saint Paul, Saint Augustine, Luther, Karl Barth, etc., and transposed into philosophic terms. But with psychoanalysis we have a completely different approach, separating from archaic drives and the pathological tendencies of archaism. It led to another turn, namely the recognition of the conflicting character of interpretation. I believe that the real turning point, almost more than the introduction of symbolism and myth, is the implacably conflicting character of interpretation. As such, this problem is going to torment me all of my life. I confronted it much later with the problem of narrative – the fact that we can tell recount very, very different things, for example concerning the French revolution. Then this notion of conflict became extremely important.

To fix a second threshold – the one that you called methodological – that was the passage from the sentence to the text – to speak in linguistic terms – where the problem of the metaphor is essentially connected to this unity of language that is the sentence. A good metaphor is a sentence, e.g., "Time is bigger." But within a text we have much wider compositions of language. That is why someone was able to observe that there was some kind of contradiction between the definition of hermeneutics that I gave at the beginning, and the one I gave later. At the beginning I said that hermeneutics is the interpretation of symbols, and then I widened the definition and said that it is the interpretation of metaphors. The introduction of the matter of the text[9] as a unity of speech that is broader than the sentence produced a sort of break. But then I was able to approach problems such as narrative, which is evidently made out of several sentences, and the problem of the composition or refiguration[10] of complexes of words. All this is very important for the conception of reality – it makes a big difference to say that reality is not only what corresponds to our sentences but what corresponds to our texts also. Here we have an element of composition, of configuration, that allows us to approach the problem of reality in terms of refiguration,

---

[9] See Paul Ricœur, *Du texte à l'action*, 112-116 (English: *From Text to Action*, 84-87); Ricoeur refers here to Gadamer's concept of "Sachlichkeit der Sprache" (Hans-Georg Gadamer, *Wahrheit und Methode*, Tübingen: Mohr, 1960/ 1990, Bd. 1, 449 ff).

[10] Paul Ricœur, *Temps et récit*, tome I: *L'intrigue et le récit philosophique* (Paris: Seuil, 1984), 144-146 [English: *Time and Narrtive*, vol. 1. Translated by Kathleen McLaughlin and David Pellauer (Chicago: University of Chicago Press, 1984), 72ff]; de idem, *Temps et récit*, tome II: *La configuration dans le récit* (Paris: Seuil, 1984), 11-16 [English: *Time and Narrtive*, vol 2. Translated by Kathleen McLaughlin and David Pellauer (Chicago: University of Chicago Press, 1985), 3-6].

with refiguration being the impact on reality of our work of configuration. This leads us to the problem, which you rightly pointed out as being a sort of "return," namely from text to action. This return is completed by the idea of refiguration, i.e., the fact that there is a sort of refiguration of reality either by metaphoric language, or by the great cultural narratives. Finally, the problem of action returned to the foreground, maybe also because of my political concerns. It is certain that I was greatly affected by the Cold War and by such important events as those that took place in Budapest. The most significant text of political philosophy that I wrote was on the Russian invasion of Hungary.

Yvanka Raynova: Are you speaking of the events of 1956-1957?

Paul Ricoeur: Yes. I asked myself questions on the role of power and the structure of power.

Yvanka Raynova: Effectively, after the Second World War this problem preoccupied philosophers more and more. You also reflected a great deal on the political positions taken up by philosophers, such as Jaspers and Heidegger. I am thinking in particular of your interview with Michel Contat in *Le Monde*, June 1987. Also, I remember especially Emmanuel Mounier's remark, in an article at the end of the forties, where he speaks of you as "a young man of Protestant formation who opens new ways to personalism." In fact, we know very little about your personal and professional relations with Mounier and the group *Esprit*, apart from the fact that you continue to contribute to its journal. Could you tell us a little more about this matter?

Paul Ricoeur: Thank you for this question. For me it is more personal than public. My friendship with Mounier was interrupted just as it began. Of course, I knew a little about Mounier when I was a student, before the war, but his ideas were in no way central to my concerns. Then, from 1940 to 1945, I was a prisoner of war. Thus I knew Mounier for only five years, from 1945 till 1950, because he died in 1950. It is during the last two years of his life that I became his philosophic co-worker on the journal. He needed a professional philosopher by his side and he thought that I could be this man. His death was, for me, devastating. I not only maintained very good relations with his successors, but our contacts became increasingly close. Some of the current team of *Esprit* were my students, for example the director of the journal, Olivier Mongin, who is going to publish a book on me in January of next year.[11] At the same time, I am not only thought of as a teacher to these followers, but also simply as a member of this community – I am the veteran, for the youngest. And I think that they are making a completely extraordinary breakthrough in the French editorial scene. I have an affinity with the young generation of *Esprit*.

Yvanka Raynova: Did you completely abandon theological hermeneutics and the problems of faith, that is to say, the "invisible path" of history and human life?[12]

---

[11] See Olivier Mongin, *Paul Ricoeur* (Paris: Seuil, 1994).
[12] See Paul Ricoeur, *Histoire et vérité* (Paris: Seuil, 1955), 81-98; English: *History and Truth*. Translated by Charles A. Kelbley (Evanston: Northwestern University Press, 1965), 81-97.

Paul Ricoeur: Not at all. But I really like to keep philosophy, as the common rational discourse, separate from my own religious, Protestant convictions that you are alluding to. At present, in the United States, the publication of a work is in progress that I made together with exegetes, and that will appear soon.[13] I am not an exegete by profession, and I depend a lot on exegetes, to know who wrote such and such a text, at which time, and for which public. What I do is in fact a philosophical reflection on biblical texts, for example on original sin or on the famous text of Exodus: "I am, who I am," or "God, why have you forsaken me," or on the laws of Sinai such as "Do not kill!" where I ask in which sense this is a law from Heaven, because it is also a human law. But I distinguish all these problems from my philosophical work, because the texts that I read are different.

Yvanka Raynova: Does that mean that your texts in *History and Truth* are not philosophical, because there are

---

[13] See André LaCocque and Paul Ricoeur, *Thinking Biblically: Exegetical and Hermeneutical Studies* (Chicago: University of Chicago Press, 1998).

many interpretations of biblical stories and quotations from the Fathers of the Church?

Paul Ricoeur: Yes indeed [hesitating for a moment], I would be schizophrenic if I had divided completely into two. I try hard to distinguish between my religious motivation and my philosophic argumentation. In my philosophical works there are no quotations of biblical texts, no references to theology; philosophy lives with its own texts. There are unifying texts, such as those on Greek tragedy, and also speculative aspects of biblical texts and this whole tradition of wisdom. I think that between the wisdom of the Middle East, expressed in the Bible, as for example in the book of *Job*, *Ecclesiastes*, *Proverbs* and maybe in the *Gospel of John* – wisdom that is not so narrative and that has many meditative sides – and my philosophical concerns are that there are necessary intersections. At the moment I work precisely on the points of intersection. The volume that is going to appear in some weeks – *Lectures 3* – contains methodological texts related to these intersection points that I try to explain.[14] Of course, in order to have points of intersection there have to be two roads...

Yvanka Raynova: At present, and especially during this meeting,[15] the problem of the Other is recognized to be a central philosophical theme. In the great philosophical debates on the Other your conception of the relation between the *Socius* and the Neighbor (*le prochain*) seems to be unique because it offers the possibility to conceive the communicative break, the reason for the lack of authentic communication (Jaspers) and intersubjectivity (Marcel), in a completely new way. Is there still a place in your current works for the Other as a Neighbor?

Paul Ricoeur: I think that it is necessary to distinguish between two notions of the Other. The Other, who has a face, can become a friend. And this is the problem of intersub-

---

[14] See Paul Ricœur, *Lectures 3. Aux frontières de la philosophie* (Paris: Seuil, 1994), 153-185, 273-326.
[15] The subject of the XIX Congress of the Fédération Internationale des Sociétés de Philosophie (FISP), which took place in Moscow (20-25 of August 1993), was "Mankind at a Turning Point: Philosophical Perspectives".

jective relations. I believe that Levinas is the thinker of this relation to *the* Other with a face. But we always have to keep in mind the relation with *an* Other, who has no face for us. For me, the Chinese somewhere over there will never become friends of mine. But I have relations to them through institutions. We have here a shift from the concept of friendship to the concept of justice. You were able to notice that my last book *Oneself as Another* puts both relations to the Other on the same level – friendship and justice. I define, moreover, the first ethical relation in the following terms: "To aim at the good life with and for others in just institutions."[16] Consequently the idea of justice concerns my relation to the Other without a face and who can forever remain without a face. It is here that the institution makes the relation, and not intersubjectivity. That is why I react against a narrow personalism that would reduce everything to the relation "I – you." There is a "you," but also an "each one."

---

[16] See Paul Ricœur, *Soi-même comme un autre* (Paris: Seuil, 1990), 202. English: *Oneself as Another*. Translated by Kathleen Blamey (Chicago: University of Chicago Press, 1992), 172.

Yvanka Raynova: Do you mean "they," *das Man*, le *on*?

Paul Ricoeur: No, "they" is anonymous, but "each one" is distributive. I believe that this is very important, because we often say: after "you" there is "they." No, there is not "they," there is "each one." And the relation of justice is: "To each his or her right." I believe that this is the category that has been neglected far too much in philosophy, especially in spiritualist philosophy, emphasizing the relations of friendship and love, but not of justice. Now it is by this that politics can be strictly connected to ethics, because politics is strictly concerned with institutions that connect individuals who will never become friends. A few will become friends, but they are correlatives of the action in an institutional frame. Whether it is the university, a company, citizenship, international institutions, or a philosophical society, I am in relation with people who are in institutional or institutionally established relations.

Yvanka Raynova: That means they are in distant relations?

Paul Ricoeur: Yes, in distant relations. It is here that the analysis of the Neighbor and the *Socius* is very important.

Yvanka Raynova: How would you assess the efforts of your former student, Enrique Dussel, concerning the awareness of the human condition in this aspect of otherness, which is one of justice? Did you not think that the understanding of oneself is not so much made "in front of the text," as you emphasized in *From Text to Action*,[17] but chiefly "in front of the Other," because before "I am" and "I think" there is the "Other," as it has been suggested by Marcel and as you seem to suggest in *Oneself as Another*?[18]

Paul Ricoeur: I do not see any contradiction. Precisely, I can associate myself entirely with the problems of Dussel through his concept of awareness (*conscientisation*). It is

---

[17] See Paul Ricœur, *Du texte à l'action*, 31, 54, 116-117 (English: *From Text to Action*, 17, 37, 97).
[18] See Paul Ricœur, *Soi-même comme un autre*, 380-393 (English: *Oneself as Another*, 329-341).

true that there is a sort of flight in front of the problems of injustice with regard to the Third World or to this "third world" that is in our home. Because the Third World is now in our home – the African Americans, the Hispanics, and the Arabs in France, etc. The Third World is not "outside," it is on the "inside" of our world. And there is a problem of victimization. I completely agree with Dussel and I do not want to magnify the problem of language. It is not by accident that I called one of my last books *From Text to Action*. At the beginning you said that there is a return to the problems in my youth – that is true, but through everything that I had learned about textuality. Now the insistence on justice and on the political dimension of inter-human relations holds an even greater and more important place, as we live in a completely fragmented and terribly dangerous world.

Yvanka Raynova: What is the reason for this or, if you want, what is the main vice of contemporary society?

Paul Ricoeur: I would say that the main vice of contemporary society is the fact that the collapse of communism in

Eastern Europe left a winner, but this winner is ill. We can now make an internal criticism of the capitalist system without being accused of being pro-communist. Things appear in the following way. The market economy is certainly the only one that is productive, that creates wealth; and at the same time this economy creates the most inequalities and injustices. Consequently, we are all in search of a combination of both the laws of the market and the intervention of the state or society to correct these inequalities. I would say that we entered an experimental period where we have to unite water and fire, because the free market presumes that there should be no intervention, but justice requires intervention. I do not believe that there is a single way. I doubt that the Third World will accept the way of the American model, for example; nor does the European world. I believe that there will be, in the future, a sort of social democracy with various combinations of the freedom of the market and the interventionism of the State. But we do not know the solution. We are going for a larger freedom than we had originally looked for, because what had been monstrous in communism is no longer an issue.

This way we are freer to make attempts, to make imaginative variations – to use the expression of Husserl – and to make combinations between the search for social justice and privatization. And it is really a very, very strong contradiction. Once again, I believe in the multiplicity of solutions.

Yvanka Raynova: In *The Conflict of Interpretations* you insist on the questioning of "I am" through "Who am I?" – a favorite question asked by Montaigne and Marcel. But it seems, nevertheless, that in *History and Truth* you had already given, if not an answer, then at least an indication, in the sense that the dialectic of history reveals a common intention towards Transcendence and shows that the human being is *Imago Dei*. Do you still support this position, or do you admit to rather a plurality of discourses on "I am" and on the question "Who am I?" i.e., a certain relativism?

Paul Ricoeur: There is no doubt that a lot of time has passed since I wrote *History and Truth*; it was about thirty years ago. And it is not only that I have changed, but also that the philosophical landscape has changed. There are no longer the same, I would not say "opponents," but the same reference points. Existentialism, Personalism and Marxism disappeared from our philosophical horizon, at least in the forms in which we knew them. I myself came to a much more complex view of the problem of "I am"; I would not say more relativist, but more inquiring. The type of philosophical discourse that I hold to, now, advantageously places the emphasis on the aporia and aporetics. The third volume of *Time and Narrative* ends with the problems that could not be resolved by the narrative – the abyssal character of time, the inapprehensible character of personal identity.[19] It is true that maybe I am going from an affirmative philosophy, self-assured, towards a much more inquiring philosophy. You can call that relativism, but personally I do not like the word "relativism," because ...

Yvanka Raynova: I did not assert it, this was only a question.

Paul Ricoeur: But the word "relativism" is contrary to "dogmatism"... It is as if there could be only one point of

---

[19] See Paul Ricœur, *Temps et récit 3. Le temps raconté* (Paris: Seuil, 1985), 349-392 [English: *Time and Narrative*, vol. 3. Translated by Kathleen McLaughlin and David Pellauer (Chicago: University of Chicago Press, 1988), 193-241].

view, and as soon as you say that there are different points of view, you are a relativist. I would prefer to introduce the word "finitude." I know that I have a limited perspective on these problems and that others have another limited perspective. I belong to a philosophical community, and I admit that there are others who see things that I do not see. It is true, you can call that "relativism," but it is also an act of reliance on the capacity of others to perceive and to understand things that I do not understand. Additionally, I would say this even for the religious tradition, if you like. A whole slice of Christianity has been expressed in the terms of Neoplatonism and this is more accessible to us now. I can thus admit that there are people who have understood things that I do not understand. I belong nevertheless to this large community where people understand or will understand things that I would never understand. *This* is what limits my own "relativism": the "relativism" of the others. [Laughter.]

Yvanka Raynova: Speaking of the Neoplatonics... You know, certainly, the Orphic myth of Dionysus-Zagreus delivered to us by Plato, where the question of the double nature of man arises. Following this myth, man is as much the image of God (even in a figurative sense) as of the Titans, i.e., of the so-called forces of the devil. All this reminds me of your subtle analysis of evil. How would you, today, after thirty or forty years, locate the problem of evil?

Paul Ricoeur: When I look back to my first education, grounded on the tradition of Saint Paul, Saint Augustine and Luther, I now consider it to be very limited. The problem of evil is that it is too strictly reduced to guilt, to the "inside." Now I am much more attentive to two things. Firstly to violence – an aspect of evil inflicted upon us by others. In the case of guilt, man torments himself through remorse. But the empire of violence is immense. The violence in the world is not simply physical – murder, homicide – there is also violence in language, in the way of writing history. There is also this "titanic" side, at which you hinted, namely auto-glorification. Secondly, the additional aspect of this is the evil of suffering. Certainly in my first works there was no place for a reflection on suffering, but only on committed evil. Now there is also the suffered evil, which is the exact opposite of violence. That is why – I do not know if you noticed this – especially since *Time and Narrative*, I always say "the acting and suffering person."[20] Narrative is a refiguration of the acting and suffering person. We can see this precisely in the Greek tragedy, which deals with greatness as well as with the fall. The tragic model, I believe, is extremely important. And moreover, the history of the Titans is connected with the archaic aspect of tragedy. We see it in *Prometheus Bound* by Aeschylus, even more than in Sophocles. With Sophocles, the tragedy of the human passions is in the center, whereas with Aeschylus we have the terrible mythical shape in others.

Yvanka Raynova: Today it is not so much narratives and myths, but history and our everyday life that brings us horrors and tragedies. Although the Cold War has ended and although we speak of a democratization of Eastern European countries, we continue to live in a world torn apart by conflicts where it often seems that we are approaching "the

---

[20] Paul Ricœur, *Temps et récit 1*, 118 (English: *Time and Narrative*, vol. 1, 60); de idem, *Temps et récit 2*, 113. See also de idem, *Soi-même comme un autre* (Paris: Seuil, 1990), 370; in the English translation this expression has been omitted [see *Oneself as Another*. Translated by Kathleen Blamey (Chicago: University of Chicago Press, 1992), 320].

25th hour of history."[21] Did you keep anything of your former "epic optimism" and faith in the final sacralization of history?[22]

Paul Ricoeur: I would say that I have abandoned more and more the idea of a philosophy of history... [thinks awhile...] I have no idea where history goes. I am more Kantian than Hegelian on this question; I ask, namely: "What should I do now?" in situations of conflict etc. But with regards to where we go, I do not know anything precise about this. What I can say is that to be responsible I do not need to have a philosophy of history. We have a very limited vision of the states of conflict, extremely limited because we are ourselves in a state of conflict, and we do not have this overhead view, this view from above. I would say, in parentheses, that present history is opaque. As for

---

[21] Paul Ricœur, *Histoire et vérité* (Paris: Seuil, 1955), 95 [English: *History and Truth*. Translated by Charles A. Kelbley (Evanston: Northwestern University Press, 1965/2007), 94]. See also Virgil Gheorghiu, *La vingt-cinquième heure*. Translated by Monique Saint-Côme and introduced by Gabriel Marcel (Paris: Plon, 1949) [English: *The twenty-fifth hour*. Translated by Rita Eldon (New York: Alfred A Knopf, 1950)].

[22] Paul Ricœur, *Histoire et vérité*, 95, 112-114 (English: *History and Truth*, 94, 110-114).

me, there is an idea of Hegel's that I wish to correct on this point, because Hegel said that we could understand an epoch only when it ended. Maybe it is only now that we can understand the period of 1917-1989, the birth of the Bolshevik revolution with all of its consequences. Whereas I do not know in which time we live now. We are in the midst of conflicts and I think that we should have an ethical rather than a speculative vision on the question "What should be done at present?"

Just now I outlined three problems. Firstly it is necessary to change the way of telling our own history and to take into account the suffering that we imposed on others – to think first of the suffering that we imposed and then to the one we ourselves underwent. This is already something that touches the way we rewrite history. Secondly, there is the question of how to combine the economic world of the market with the obligation of justice towards the poorest. We do not know the solution for it, but it is a task. Thirdly, avoid nuclear war, which always remains a possibility. I do not know whether this is just a fantasy, but I am now afraid of the possibility of atomic wars in the Third World. They are in no way excluded. It is still possible that one day a country in Africa or Asia will use nuclear extortion on another country. It will then become a problem for the international community, who will have an obligation to resolve the matter. We have at present the duty to give to the international community the means of intervention, but always supported by an extremely strong legality. The construction of an international law endowed with agents of force and intervention..., it is certainly a task. We are at present in a learning process with Iraq, Somalia, Bosnia, and we can see that we always begin with errors. We are in a period of learning where there is no longer a fight between two blocs, but a polycentrism from which the international community should gain a general will and endow it at the same time with instruments of rights and with instruments of intervention.

Yvanka Raynova: Does that mean that it is crucial to establish an international government, which would help to resolve the problems of our contemporary world?

Paul Ricoeur: No, I do not think so. Our problem is unprecedented, because we have, for subjects concerning right/rights and force, only national countries. Our task thus is not to create an international entity that would be the Nation State of force "X." Now we have a completely new reality that should form something like a "concert of nations."

Yvanka Raynova: This is what I wanted to say when thinking of the federation envisaged by Camus.

Paul Ricoeur: I think that, from this point of view, it is Kant who saw things most clearly, in his project of eternal peace as a consequence of *ius gentium*, of human rights. I think that it is necessary for us to go down this road, because it is much more difficult to arrive at a concert of nations than end in a power of a nation. Now we are put in danger as much by the division of the nations as by the ascendancy of a single force, that is to say, by world chaos and by the American monocracy. Moreover, the Americans themselves have some difficulty in situating themselves, because the other countries oblige them to play the role of policeman of the world, often even against their own will.

Yvanka Raynova: Could we also accept that Lyotard is right when he notes that there is no real solution to current conflicts, because in every "solution" is but one of the parts of the discourse that imposes its own idiom on the others?

Paul Ricoeur: No, I think this point of view is too extreme. What I want to say is that we have an historic experience of compromise and negotiations. In public activities, we collide all the time with the negotiations between leaders and administrative advisers, etc. The democracies, which today function well, to a certain extent, are established on compromises such as the rights of minorities, the constitutional control of the ruling majority, etc. It is exactly this historic experience of compromise which needs to be widened. To honor the *différend*, is to see the reality such as it is, but it does not mean in any way that it has a necessary existence, it is just a fact. To say that the *différend* has the last word would be a surrender. In fact, the *différend* is only part of the problem.

Yvanka Raynova: Even if just solutions were found, do you think that philosophy, especially political philosophy and discursive ethics, such as have been presented to us by Karl-Otto Apel, for example, have the necessary instruments to succeed in solving the problems in practice?

Paul Ricoeur: What Apel offers is not politics but a reflection on the conditions of consensus, which allows us to better take into account the differences. Because, what is a *différend* if not the insoluble character of a conflict which nevertheless aims at an ideal consensus? But, if you do not look for an ideal consensus, then you are completely indifferent to this *différend*. The task is to make our common existence possible. Here also I am Kantian. In the paragraph on the philosophy of right in *The Metaphysics of Morals*, Kant lays out the project of the conciliation between politics and free will. He begins with a certain historic pessimism, which comes from what he describes as "*ungesellige Gesellschaft*." This is the situation; the task, however, is to reconcile the contradictions.

Yvanka Raynova: Well, how can political *philosophy* reconcile them, when it has no power over real politics?

Paul Ricoeur: As I have just said – political philosophy is not politics. Politics is bound to force and to power, to the relations between power and right. It leads to the problem of creativity and public opinion. We arrive, in the final account, at the eighteenth century concept of *Öffentlichkeit*. It is at this level that we solve the problems of philosophy. At the moment we contribute, you and I, to public opinion, to the debate, and to the discussion.

Yvanka Raynova: And do you think that such debates will change anything? Recently a German politician expressed the somewhat cynical opinion, which is regrettably a fact, that "politics is not made on the streets," that is, in the *Öffentlichkeit*, or even in philosophical discourses.

Paul Ricoeur: I believe, rather, in the modest language of Rorty, in the fact that we can be good intermediaries between different traditions by clarifying each one through the others. I believe that we are useful, at this level – requiring better arguments from our opponents. Apel said something on this point that is full of drive, namely that there is an ethics of discussion. If there is not, it is because we reside simply in relations of force. Certainly, discussion alone cannot resolve the relations of force, but it obliges force to put itself onto the plane of discourse.

Yvanka Raynova: So do you believe that philosophy can contribute to changing the world?

Paul Ricoeur: [Resolutely] *I don't know!* But I do know what I have to do.

2. All that gives rise to thought

Yvanka Raynova: When reading *The Conflict of Interpretations* we get the impression that for you the fundamental philosophical problem is, as for Heidegger, that of being, approached by a hermeneutics of being-in-the-world. But is this mediation between the philosophy of being and the philosophy of language, which needs to begin from the text[23] and from the center of the language and the sense always there,[24] not ultimately a neglecting, if not a "forgetting," of the problem of the meaning of being and consequently of existence and the lived experience, in favor of the text?

Paul Ricoeur: I would say that there are two exits out of the text in my own philosophy. Firstly, the fact that the text is not closed in itself, and secondly and most importantly, the question: "what sort of world is opened by a text?" Moreover, this notion of the "world of the text,"[25] which I

---

[23] Paul Ricœur, *Du texte à l'action*, 30-31 (English: *From Text to Action*, 17-18).
[24] Paul Ricœur, *Le conflit des interprétations* (Paris: Seuil, 1969), 283 [English: *The Conflict of Interpretations: Essays in hermeneutics* (Evanston, Illinois: Northwestern University Press, 1974), 285].
[25] See Paul Ricœur, *Du texte à l'action*, 112-116 (English: *From Text to Action*, 84-87); de idem, *Temps et récit*, tome III, 284-288 (English:

have in common with Gadamer, already marks an ontological orientation of the analysis of the text. And it is because of this that I left behind structuralism, which forbids, in a sense, all that is extra-linguistic. My profound conviction was always that language is not about itself, but about what is, including fictional language, which at first sight seems to have little to do with things other than itself. The meaning of fiction is also to propose a possible world, and thence a virtual ontology. That is my first answer. As for my second answer, it is that the text is not alone, it has a reader. And the reader brings with him a lived experience and some expectations, *Erwartungen*. Consequently the reader brings *his* world to the text. Reading is an act that puts the world of the text into conflict with the world of the reader. This way there is an ontological dimension on the side of the author, opened up by the text, and on the other hand a confrontation of the reader with the world of the text.

Time and Narrative, vol. 3, 157-161); cf. de idem, *La métaphore vive* (Paris: Seuil, 1975), 61 [English: *The Rule of Metaphor: Multi-Disciplinary Studies in the Creation of Meaning in Language*. Translated by Robert Czerny, Kathleen McLaughlin and John Costello (London: Routledge and Kegan Paul, 1978), 48].

Yvanka Raynova: But is the text sufficient to render the world of the one who speaks or who writes? Because my life is not a story, it is not a text, as Gabriel Marcel put it,[26] and consequently the text or the story can never render all the richness of our lived experience.

Paul Ricoeur: In the conferences that I have just given here on memory and history, I proceed entirely in this direction. I tried to rise beyond the narrative text towards the lived memory and beyond the memory, which is already a sort of speech that is held unto itself, in the direction of lived experience.[27] It is life that deploys a deep temporality. And it is this deep temporality that creates the fact that there is a history of a life before the story. I proceed completely in the direction of Gabriel Marcel, in that my life is not a story. But the story is the story of my life. There is a

---

[26] Gabriel Marcel, *Etre et Avoir*, vol. 1 (Paris: Aubier, 1968), 11-14; de idem, *Le mystère de l'Etre*, vol. 1 (Paris: Aubier, 1951), 163-185.
[27] See Paul Ricœur, *La mémoire, l'histoire, l'oubli* (Paris: Seuil, 2000), 456 [English: *Memory, History, Forgetting*. Translated by Kathleen Blamey and David Pellauer (Chicago: University of Chicago Press, 2004), 349].

sort of ontological priority of life, if there is an epistemological priority of the story.

The more we insist on the character of linguistic, narrative, and textual mediation, the more we are urged to rediscover what is behind these mediations of the immediate. I return to this notion of life, which concerns me more and more, because it is the problem which I find in ethics: before the memory of the duty, there is an ethics of the good life. And thus I find the notion of life not only as a biological phenomenon, but also as that of being, plunged between birth and death as a space to be cultivated and reflected upon. I think of the expression of Socrates, when he says that an unexamined life is not worth living. When we emphasize examination, then we are in a philosophy of meditation, of language etc., but it is also necessary to emphasize the word "life" because what is to be examined is precisely a life. The cohesion of a life is precisely what is in search of a story. The demand for a story comes from the depths of life in order to clarify itself.

Yvanka Raynova: In *From Text to Action* you say that it is the "matter" of the text as the object of the hermeneutics that configures our world.[28] But should we not begin rather with the being-in-the-world in order to arrive at the text, as you suggest in *The Conflict of Interpretations*?[29] In other words, why does hermeneutic phenomenology become more and more a hermeneutics of texts and not of existence?

Paul Ricoeur: All our difficulties in this discussion come from the fact that on the one hand we are living beings among other living beings, but that on the other hand we are living beings which have this specificity as speaking subjects. There is no human experience that is not structured by language. I say that even for the most primitive feelings, such as those described by Heidegger – fear, fright, enjoyment and even human desire. I am going to offer an example that is at first sight unfavorable, but which I would like to pull in this direction. All psychoanalysis is directed towards the libido, to the deep aspects of sexuality etc. But if psychoanalysis is possible at all, it is just be-

---

[28] Paul Ricœur, *Du texte à l'action*, 125-126 (English: *From Text to Action*, 95-96).
[29] Paul Ricœur, *Le conflit des interprétations*, 261 (English: *The Conflict of Interpretations*, 259).

cause the libido speaks. It can only be approached when it rises to the level of language, because it ascends to language. Now this language is a common language. In the secret of the heart, if we use words to structure our fears, our desires etc., we use the language that belongs to everyone. That is why we can say that public language is in the center of our solitude.

Yvanka Raynova: But if we accept that all experience is structured by language, then how can we explain the "unspoken" and the unspeakable, all that we cannot express by words, by language? Too often there is something unsaid and unspeakable, in our lived experience and in our relations with others...

Paul Ricoeur: It is the limit of language. I am completely aware that it is a claim: the claim to be the chief of the senses and to govern its own life at the level of all these mediations, which, moreover, go beyond language, to society, politics and power. It is always necessary to return to the root of all this – to life. But life is nothing if it is not a life-with. Now, as soon as we go into the life-with, into the life together with others, we are in daily linguistic practice. You should not think that language is always structured by logic; language is also the daily practice of exchange with others, the simple dialogical dimension.

Yvanka Raynova: Does this mean that the limit of language is also in a certain sense the limit of knowledge?

Paul Ricoeur: Yes. But I retained your idea of the "unsaid." It is not accidental that in the unsaid we have the said; but we put it negatively, which is to know that not everything passes through language. At the same time, the unsaid is an invitation to say or to respect the unspoken. There is a whole aspect of what we might call abstinence, i.e., the respect for a secret. It is good, also, that not everything is said. We are sent here in another way to say that which is stated to ourselves, the said of the meditation, of personal confession or rumination.

Yvanka Raynova: You mean the said "in thought," mentally...

Paul Ricoeur: Yes, I think that Plato was right to say that the most personal, the most secret thought is a sort of dialogue with ourselves. There is, moreover, the French expression "*for intérieur*," which I like very much and which is derived from 'forum.'[30] There is a sort of private forum where we are two, even when alone.

Yvanka Raynova: Then the limit of language is not necessarily a limit of knowledge, because we can feel, for example, whether the other loves us or not, even if he or she does not say it. We can intuitively conceive of things that are not expressed by language. Possibly the most important things in life take place in silence and not in language, and maybe the highest knowledge arises from listening to "the voice of silence."[31]

Paul Ricoeur: There is a lower limit – the limit of what does not pass into language from life. There is an upper

---

[30] See Paul Ricœur, *Réflexion faite. Autobiographie intellectuelle* (Paris: Editions Esprit, Seuil, 1995), 107.
[31] See Helena Petrovna Blavatsky, *The Voice of the Silence; being Chosen Fragments from the: "Book of the Golden Precepts"* (London; New York: The Theosophical Publishing Co. Ltd., 1889).

limit – the mystical experience; this means that, beyond language as mostly articulated by philosophy and theology, there is silence. We also have a similarity: silence at the beginning and silence at the end. And then there is a lateral limit – it is the relation with the other, where we have the unsaid of love and friendship. That is the secret. There are, as a matter of fact, three "unsaids": the one which precedes us, the one which exceeds us, and the one which proceeds toward us.

Yvanka Raynova: You explain your famous sentence, "The symbol gives rise to thought," in the following way: "The symbol (…) is what gives sense; but what it gives is something for thought, something to think about (...). Our judgment thus suggests that everything is already said in an enigma, and nevertheless that it is ever to begin and re-begin everything in the perspective of thought."[32] It seems also that philosophy begins as *thought* and not as *text*. What

---

[32] Paul Ricœur, *Le conflit des interprétations*, 284 [English: "The Hermeneutics of Symbols and Philosophical reflection." Translated by Denis Savage (in Don Ihde, ed., *The Conflict of Interpretations: Essays in hermeneutics*. Evanston, Illinois: Northwestern University Press, 1974), 299].

is the exact relation between thought, language and text as the written language? Is there a primacy of thought over language, or rather, a simultaneity?

Paul Ricoeur: There are two answers. The first is that we do not know any state of thought which is outside language. However, this is not a prison, because there are so many different forms of language – scientific, aesthetic, literary, everyday, and mystic. It is necessary to *redistribute* the spaces of language differently, in order to see that thought is coextensive with language. The second answer is that there is also a phenomenon, which seems to me particularly important: that of the phenomenon of the plurality of languages. I find that we have not reflected on this enough. Because, when we say "thought and language," it is necessary to say that thought *is* language. We discover what thought is in a very important act, which is the act of translating. Here I am, after all, speaking to somebody who knows very well what this means. [Smiles.] By this act we see that we have no other resources we can draw on, for thinking what has been said in a text, but to say it in another text. And when we say that a translation is a "good translation," we mean that in this text the thought is the same as the one in the other text. But at the same time we have no means of verifying the identity of meaning in the two texts, because there is no third text, which would, in a sense, be a text without text. All we have is the hard and painful work of continual correction to our translation by way of 'living' the foreign language, while at the same time 'receiving' it in our home like a host. I believe that here we have an experience of linguistic hospitality which is, in fact, the experience of the superiority of thought over language, but a superiority which shows itself only in the work of working one language into another.

Yvanka Raynova: Yes, but you say in *From Text to Action* that speech (*la parole*) always relates to a previous text, which it then interprets. Is there really a superiority of text over speech?

Paul Ricoeur: I am persuaded that writing is a fundamental phenomenon. If laws were not written, we would have the arbitrary power of a judge. How would our feelings be experienced if they were not written down in poems, novels, or in epics? Writing is the grand medium of communication. But, on the other hand, humans spoke before they wrote, only – they certainly did not leave any trace of this. Writing is a registered speech. I believe that it is necessary to protect this dialectics of speech and writing without giving any priority to the one or the other. We have historical examples of the superiority of speech over writing, when writing was in decline – that of Plato's reminiscences and that of Rousseau's feelings. Nevertheless, Plato writes them down, and so does Rousseau, and we would not know of their pleas against writing if they had not written them down. This is a paradox too. As Gadamer observed quite precisely, it is writing which gives duration and universality to speech. According to this famous sentence, speech flies away and the writing remains.[33] There is a fragility in speech, which makes it such that writing, by extending material support to it, gives it a sort of second chance.

Yvanka Raynova: I asked this question, because there is a text in which you vigorously support the superiority of text

---

[33] *Verba volant, scripta manent.*

over speech. More concretely, you say the following: "And yet the initial hermeneutical situation of Christian preaching would be missed if the relation between speech and writing were not posited at the very origin of every problem of interpretation. At all these stages, speech maintains a relation to writing: first it is related to an earlier writing that it interprets; Jesus himself interpreted the Torah; St. Paul and the author of the Letter to the Hebrews interpreted the Christic event in light of the prophecies and institutions of the old covenant. More generally, a hermeneutics of the Old Testament, considered as a given set of writings, is implied in the proclamation that Jesus is the Christ... It therefore appears that writing must precede speech, if speech is not to remain a *cry*."[34]

Paul Ricoeur: This is probably a little excessive... This is a text that reacts against something in Protestant theology which I called the emphasis on speech. But I have a much more balanced text, which is published in *Lectures 3* and which is entitled "The tangle of speech and writing."[35] And

---

[34] Paul Ricœur, *Du texte à l'action*, 124 (*From Text to Action*, 93-94).
[35] Paul Ricœur, "L'enchevêtrement de la voix et de l'écrit dans le

I recognize myself much more in that text. I demonstrate therein that we are always in a state of coming and going, because, when believers speak of "God Talk," they immediately bring out the Holy Bible. From where do we know about this "God's Talk," other than from the Holy Bible? Or we have a personal fusion with the Holy Spirit. It is true that Western theology neglected this aspect of the theology of the Holy Spirit to a great degree, which would probably raise the equilibrium between writing and speech, but no doubt attended by all the dangers of the charismatic, of the personal fusion with the Holy Spirit of people who say: "I carry the Holy Spirit with me, it is what inspires me," etc. It is a matter of fact that the Christian tradition has found its stability in the canon of the Bible; the Jews also established a biblical canon, actually there were two. There is, after all, a delimited body of writing which is a topic of reference for various traditions. Even in the text which you quoted in a critical way, with reason, there is a projection which restores the advantage of speech. At the end there is a movement between the registered speech and the speech that is

---

discours biblique," in idem, *Lectures 3*. Paris: Seuil, 1994), 307-326.

once more liberated by the projection. I cannot escape this dialectical relation, where speech precedes writing, and writing, which, when it does not precede the word, then it at least protects it.

Yvanka Raynova: During our first conversation in Moscow you said that you prefer to distinguish philosophy – as universal and rational speech – from your religious belief, and that you made this distinction between philosophy and religion as "reading completely different texts." My question is, is it really the reading of philosophical texts that characterizes an analysis as philosophical, and which would then be the difference between a reading of philosophical texts and a reading of religious texts? Is it not possible for these analyses to be made on one and the same text with several readings or interpretations – philosophical, psychological, theological, etc.?

Paul Ricoeur: I continue to protect the autonomy of philosophy, firstly because the founding texts of philosophy in no way have the canonical character of a religious or denominational confession. They are open to everybody;

there is no Church around a philosophical text. And then secondly, they constitute a language of communication between believer and unbeliever. For this reason I maintain, fundamentally, the autonomy of philosophy. After all, St Thomas Aquinas did the same, in the Middle Ages, and then Descartes, Kant and all the great philosophers who were also religious. This is my first answer. And to give a second answer, I will just say that today, that is at the end of my life, I am keen on typing up both kinds of discourse. And all I work on at present is about the intersection of religious and philosophical discourse. I shall quote three examples. Firstly, what I wrote on the relation between love and justice. Love has a religious source, in the widest sense; it is the sacred of the human person and it speaks poetically. But it acts on justice by asking it to be more just, more universal, more respectful to persons. In this way justice, which has been a fundamental philosophical subject since Socrates, Plato and Aristotle, right up to Kant and Hegel, is always under the eye, the pressure and the inspiration of love. Here is one intersection. The second example: in my philosophy of language I always held in reserve the question of the origin of language. And everything tends to show that language precedes itself, so that the idea of an origin of language escapes us completely. Not only because in our private life others spoke to us before we spoke, because we are not the first ones to speak – for we are at first involved in listening before being involved in speech – but also because the great founding texts of culture put language in an inaccessible place of origin, which has the function of a limit, in order to protect this origin of language. I shall say that here we have another relation between religion and philosophy – the sacred dimension of founding language and the logical and interlocutory character of language, either in its scientific or in its historic shape, in brief, the profane practice of language. So the relation between the sacred and the profane in language is another point of intersection. And the third topic that I am investigating is that of the memory, by showing that before the history of the historians there is personal memory, and before that there is life and living together. This living together is based on a sort of primitive gift, on generosity, which makes possible the act of confidence in language, which itself is based on the founding language of any language. You see that I am completely sensitive to finding an intersection between these two usages of thought – philosophical and religious thought.

Yvanka Raynova: All right, but what is the *differentia specifica* of philosophical discourse in contrast to religious or theological discourse?

Paul Ricoeur: Firstly, it is what differentiates texts. The texts of Plato, Aristotle, Kant or Hegel are philosophical texts. Why? Because they belong to no sect, no school, nor to anything that ressembles a church. I believe that it is up to a religious language to be the founder of an ecclesial community. There is an ecclesiological dimension, not necessarily in the institutional sense constrained by hierarchy, priests, bishops etc., but in the sense of a specific community. This very particular mode of living together is based on texts and religious speech. There we find the above-mentioned problem of translation in the sense that religion does not exist other than in religions and in the problem of communication between the different religions. This problem has no analogy in philosophy. There is a plurality of religious confessions that creates a similar problem to the one that I called linguistic hospitality, and which is, in a sense, an ecumenical hospitality.

Yvanka Raynova: But Plato was not without a confession, he was initiated in the Greek mysteries. Like Pythagoras, he protected the secret of initiation because he was obliged to do so, but his philosophy is perhaps the exoteric and stylized expression of an esoteric knowledge propagated by a "secret society." We know also that many philosophers were part of Masonic lodges and adapted the principles of Freemasonry to their philosophy. Is it "membership in a sect" which is the true demarcation line between religion and philosophy? Is it not rather the *approach* to the problems of a text and the reading of it?

Paul Ricoeur: I insist upon the intersections. We can arrive at a philosophical reading of religious texts. Let us, for example, take the book of Job, which can serve as a whole philosophical reflection on evil. Of the *Song of Songs* we can make a reflection on the relation between the erotic and charity. We can make a reflection on the laws of Moses with regard to the Kantian imperative. Thus cross-reading can take place in both directions. But you asked me another question, whether there was a specific difference. I see the specific difference in the way these texts are received and transmitted.

Yvanka Raynova: I see in this intersection between philosophy and religious thought two paths that cross, but that do so in order to keep their distance.[36] It seems to me that through the years this distance has become greater in your writings. While at the beginning you were inspired by the religious philosophies of Gabriel Marcel and Karl Jaspers, and spoke about the necessity of a "second Copernican revolution" that would put Transcendence into the center,

---

[36] See: Yvanka Raynova, "Entre la régression et l'eschatologie: Philosophie et théologie dans la phénoménologie herméneutique de Paul Ricœur," in Charlotte Methuen, ed., *Time – Utopia – Eschatology* (Leuven: Peeters, 1999), 65-80; This study was originally published in 1994 as "La distinction entre philosophie et theologie chez Paul Ricœur" in the Journal of the Bulgarian Society for francophone Philosophy and Culture (see *Anthropos*, 1994/3-4, 28-49) and Paul Ricoeur knew about it. See also in German, de idem, "Philosophischer und theologischer Diskurs in der hermeneutischen Phänomenologie Paul Ricoeurs," *Divinatio* 14 (Autumn–Winter 2001): 67-86.

as the horizon of subjectivity, as a *presence* upsetting the theory of the subject,[37] in your later works, Transcendence is only an "aporia of the Other" where "philosophical discourse comes to an end."[38] Is a religious philosophy still possible from this last perspective?

Paul Ricoeur: We should return to the beginning. I was confronted from the start with the polarity between philosophy and religion, at first because Gabriel Marcel was quite anxious to distinguish between what was religious from what was philosophical in his thought. Jaspers was not a Christian, and what he calls the philosophical faith is not a confessional faith. On the other hand, from the beginning I was concerned myself with critical thinking, because my work for my diploma, as a young man, was on the French Neo-Kantians Lachelier and Lagneau, and thus I was confronted with this plurality. It is only now, at the end of my life, that I am preoccupied with the intersections between critical thinking, in the broad sense of the word and

---

[37] Paul Ricœur, *Philosophie de la volonté. Le volontaire et l'involontaire* (Paris: Aubier, 1949), 443-456.
[38] Paul Ricœur, *Soi-même comme un autre*, 409 (English: *Oneself as Another*, 355).

not only in a criticist Kantian sense, and religious thinking. But I insist upon a further aspect, namely, I am interested in the sapiential aspects of biblical thought. It should be noted that I use the word 'thought' for the Bible. I shall add, within brackets, that I have never believed that philosophy is the only way of thinking. There is thought outside of philosophy, but there is also some thought that reflects on the human condition in the Bible, often even under appearances that are completely alien to thought, like the long stories of the *Book of Kings*, or *Proverbs* or the *Psalms*. It is a way of implementing thought that has its own rules and its own rhetoric, and that is different from philosophical argumentation. So, to answer your question, I cannot say that I have passed from a time when I was immersed in religious thought to a time when I was divided; actually I am more attentive to the intersections, to the exchanges, but it was constantly a problem for me to protect these polarities while at the same time investigating the regions of intersection.

Yvanka Raynova: I know that you demonstrated this very well in *Lectures 3*, where you show that philosophy has to do with Being, from where it can be raised to the Divine, and that religion has to do with God, which makes it so that we can pass from one to the other: from the Divine to God and vice versa.[39] But my question does not refer to this passage, nor to the possibilities of investigating intersections, which you have already demonstrated. The question which preoccupies me is this: are there possibilities of having a religious *philosophy* – here I put the emphasis on philosophy – and *religious* philosophy, that is, possibilities to arrive at a sort of synthesis and not just of investigating the intersections between *two* paths, which cross somewhere. In other words, are we able to elaborate in a philosophical way, using a philosophical method and philosophical arguments, the subjects and problems of faith, by beginning with its perspectives – those of Transcendence (God) and the Sacred – which would cease to be a "stop" for philosophy, but rather a starting point?

Paul Ricoeur: I would like to complicate your question before answering it. Firstly there are several philosophies, and we are confronted with a fragmentation of philosophi-

---

[39] Paul Ricœur, *Lectures 3*, 184-185.

cal questioning. If we are not Hegelian, we are not in a regime of totalization. I shall say the same thing about religion, not only because there are several religions and in fact several denominations within Christianity, but also because the biblical world is not a unified world. There are several competing theologies at work in the same field of biblical writings. Firstly, the Christians are heirs to Jewish thought, thus there already has been some sort of first conflict between the inheritance from the Jews and the innovation, the Christian "good news." But the Jewish inheritance is a multiple inheritance. If we take two extremes, for example *Leviticus*, with its detailed prescriptions on food and clothing, etc., and the *Song of Songs*, which is a sort of liberated glorification of beauty and love, then we are confronted with two poles. There is no thought that could combine all of this, because we have already two domains split up within themselves and, for a stronger reason, because they intersect. This is what I learned from hermeneutic thought, it is a fact that we always aim at totality and unity as a horizon, but that our thought always remains fragmentary. That means that we cannot transform this horizon into a possession.

Yvanka Raynova: All right, I agree that in this plurality of thoughts we have only *variations* of religious philosophy. But do you think that it is possible to use the method of hermeneutic phenomenology, in order to elaborate just such a variant of religious philosophy?

Paul Ricoeur: I would be much closer to you on this point. But I would like to return to the expression "religious philosophy," with which I do not feel at ease. By this term we can designate two things: on the one hand, a philosophy that has a religious component or aim, in which religion is absolutely inherent, and on the other hand, a philosophy *of* religion.

Yvanka Raynova: I did not mean to pose the question of the philosophy of religion.

Paul Ricoeur: Exactly, I just wanted to push it aside. Also, I was interested in the philosophy of religion, for example in Kant's *Religion within the Limits of Reason Alone*, in a philosophy of mythology, in Schelling's philosophy of revelation, etc. What you call "religious philosophy" is a philosophy that has an opening toward religion. But I shall, at the same time, resist the identification of a God who is named and who is prayed to in the *Psalms* and in the prophecies, with the word 'God' in philosophy, which is the presupposition of a particular culture that is no longer ours. Let us take, for example, Descartes, who says: "The Perfect, that is God." Here we are in a culture for which there is no doubt that we speak about the same thing when we speak of the highest Idea in philosophy – the Idea of Infinity, of Being, of the Perfect – and God. We are heirs to a culture that has been fragmented, and this dissociation is beneficial in the sense that we have a better awareness of the fact that what we name "God" in philosophy is not somebody to whom we can pray, it is not somebody with whom we can enter into a personal relation, but a *concept*. I have taken three examples, namely the idea of Infinity, of Being and of the Perfect, because indeed they approach very closely that which is called "God" in the Bible, but also because a shock went through church and prophecy on philosophy. I think, for example, of St Thomas Aquinas who strayed from Aristotle as a philosopher precisely because he was Christian, because his Christian faith made him attentive to a sort of deviation, to a bifurcation on the inside of the idea of Being; the most common notion of Being is, at the same time, the act of being. Etienne Gilson emphasized, in particular, this character by saying that, when St Thomas Aquinas speaks about the act of being it is a sort of shadow thrown by Christianity on the pure philosophical idea of Being. We have no reason to think that, when Aristotle employs the word "being" he thinks of God: on the contrary, the tendency of historians would be to say that Aristotle's final religion was rather an astral religion, a cosmic religion of fixed spheres. And when he uses the word "God" in the singular, he says that God attracts us toward him, but that he does not act on us; this is the attraction of an object of love. Thus, there is a simlarity and at the same time an immense difference between these two conceptions. For a stronger reason, if you follow the development from Descartes onwards, you will see that the religious element of the idea of Infinity gets closer to mathematics. It is especially Pascal who was very sensitive to the fact that the God of the philosophers is *not* the God of Abraham, Isaac and Jacob. Actually, the critique of ontotheology, especially prominent in some Post-Heideggerian circles, is a sort of warning against a mixture, or an identification of the idea of Being with that of God. Culturally we find ourselves at present in this moment of separation. I think, particularly concerning the philosophy of culture, that because there were other periods in which philosophers were much more sensitive to the deep coherence between the Greek philosophical inheritance and the theological Hebraic or Christian inheritance; there was an age of integration, and we are now in an age of disintegration. But we did not choose the time in which we live; we belong to a divided culture in which we have to live as best we can. That is why I say that the problem of confusion must be replaced by the problem of intersections.

Yvanka Raynova: Does that mean that you deny even the possibility of a religious philosophy of the type of Edith Stein or Simone Weil?

Paul Ricoeur: I like your references very much. But if we take Edith Stein, for example, we see that by being converted to Catholicism she adopted Thomism. That means that for her it is obvious that the God of the philosophers is the same as the God of Catholicism.

Yvanka Raynova: All right, the Catholic perspective can seem narrow; it was narrow even for Edith Stein, who did not feel very comfortable with Thomism, especially at the beginning. It also explains why Simone Weil stayed outside of the church, and it is not incidental that in her *Cahiers* she uses examples from different religions and traditions. But let us take Teilhard de Chardin, who elaborated a religious philosophy that deviated from the Catholic canon. Or Emmanuel Mounier – *Esprit* was founded as a community of philosophers and religious thinkers belonging to different confessions. There were -you know this better than I – Catholics, Protestants, Orthodox, Hindus, even Atheists, united by a common spiritual platform. Mounier's philosophy was very open; it had welcomed not only various religious perspectives but also a sort of socialism. All this seems forgotten, and for many even irrelevant to the present day, but what have you got to say about a phenomenology with religious orientation, of Levinas' type?

Paul Ricoeur: His ideas are indeed going to leak out towards this deep unity that you seek. I told him that he went further than I, but in the specific sense of extending me, in the sense that what is said in passing suddenly becomes a sort of opening. I am, in a certain sense, also very keen to unify myself and not to stay in division, but I am constrained by my fear of confusion.

Yvanka Raynova: There are significant reasons and arguments in favor of this approach: We know from Brentano how important it is not to merge philosophy and religion, or to subordinate philosophy to theology. And as someone who lived under a totalitarian regime I know how important it is, not to allow philosophy to be subjected to other disciplines or institutions through ideology or politics. But the question here is to know whether a philosopher, who is at the same time a believer, can develop his vision of the world (*Weltanschauung*), which is so very different from that of an unbeliever, in a philosophical conception. In other words, could we, without mixing philosophy and religion, make *philosophy* by preserving the dimension of "beyond," of the Invisible and Transcendence? Let us put aside Catholicism and Christianity. We have various examples of Hinduism connecting philosophy and religion; we have Buddhist philosophy and even Zen-Buddhist readings of Heidegger. Or let us take Pythagoras, Plato and the Neoplatonists, whose philosophical systems were magnificent syntheses of metaphysical, ethical and political ideas.

Paul Ricoeur: I completely agree with you that it is necessary to keep these great examples as something more than nostalgia for a lost era, namely, as a reminder of the fundamental task that is the projection of a horizon. Whilst we cannot repeat the deep unity experienced by Pythagoras, Plato and the Neoplatonists, we can remember it. And it is here that I would like to evoke a category that I utilize somewhere else, that of "the unkept promise"; because Pythagorism and Platonism promised something that they were not able to deliver, namely a religion which would bring together all people. They excluded the mysteries and popular cults and remained something like a society of the initiated. All the thoughts of the Neoplatonics remain, if not in a secret society, then in a society of thought, and not in the total shape of an integrated society. It was the Middle Ages that tried to realize an integrated society; but all historians tell us that the Middle Ages dreamt of much more than was ever realized. I am very interested in the studies of the French historian Le Goff,[40] who showed that all modern institutions were in fact created in the Middle Ages. It is all these institutions that made the unity burst. In this way arose the civil power of municipalities, the trade power of the merchants, the universities, which were different from convents; we have, even on the inside of a religious order, a plurality, a competition between religious orders, yet the religious authority is not absolutely unified. We can clearly see the roots of the explosion grounded in the medieval dream of unification. It is in a certain kind of revival that we came closer to this integration. Two days ago I saw, in the museum of Capodimonte, with what ease painters passed from profane to religious subjects: a vio-

---

[40] Jacques Le Goff, *L'imaginaire médiéval* (Paris: Gallimard), 1985 [English: *The Medieval Imagination*. Translated by Arthur Goldhammer (Chicago: The University of Chicago Press, 1988)].

lated Lucretia who stabs herself, and then, close to her, a Magdalene in ecstasy. These two figures – Lucretia, the violated Roman, and then Magdalene, the repentant prostitute – are two emblematic figures which speak to us of lost unity, yet from the point of view of a fragmentary vision. And I think that this is our condition. The last attempt was that of Hegel, who is the only one who has attempted totally to combine religious philosophy or the philosophy of religion within the philosophy of spirit. But at what cost? At the cost, exactly, of reducing religion to a gnosis, that is, to a wisdom that ignores its own rules, that ignores what is figurative in an abstract thought. Then it *is* necessary to have a philosopher to tell religion what it is without knowing it. Thus I find that there is much more violence in this integration of religion with philosophy than in the recognition of their specificity and the specificity of their intersections.

Yvanka Raynova: Does this mean that philosophy has to be an assembling of "everybody," rather than an association of the "initiated"?

Paul Ricoeur: To begin with, philosophy is the result of an inheritance and this inheritance has a finite cultural configuration. Philosophy is not the whole of thinking; it stopped integrating the sciences, economics, the humanities, etc. In my opinion, our problem is always a problem of collecting what erupts, and of accepting the condition of dispersion that is much more ancient and primitive, and that results from the fact that human thought is finite, and that it does not reach the abyss of Being in a unifying vision. This unifying vision is approached by a series of approximations or, to use the Leibnizian vocabulary, by perspectives and fragments of perspectives, something that we aim for, but that we will never reach.

Yvanka Raynova: We have a similar problem with Justice. In your book *The Just* you start with Rawls, but you proceed, at the same time, beyond his perspective.[41] What issue would you address if we were instead to start with Lyo-

---

[41] Paul Ricoeur, *Le Juste* (Paris: Editions Esprit, Le Seuil, 1995), 71-120, 220-221 [English: *The Just*. Translated by David Pellauer (Chicago: University of Chicago Press, 2000), 36-75, 155-156].

tard's ethics of justice that is not satisfied, either with a theory of contract, or with a conception of consensus?

Paul Ricoeur: Yes, I began with Rawls. But when we quote Rawls, we always quote *A theory of Justice*, which appeared in 1972, and that was 25 years ago. Later on, Rawls published an entire *oeuvre*. Today you heard the usage I made of the concept of "reasonable discord" that is exactly the abandonment of the concept of consensus. Rawls is completely aware that only a certain number of societies that reached a kind of political maturity would entertain his theory of justice. In other words, the theory of justice is, as Rawls himself says, a theory that succeeds the great contractualism. Now, what characterizes contractualist philosophy is the fact that it takes place outside of history. But in his last works Rawls was very sensitive to the conditions of application for his theory of justice. When I began to present Rawls, I always presented the arguments against him, to show that we cannot pass directly from an ahistoric theory of contract to the conditions of its execution. Now, the last Rawls book responded precisely to these objections, in particular by saying that only a type of culture could realize its ideal of justice that is – I would add, roughly speaking – the ideal of social democracy, that is a market economy combined with a distributive politics of justice. It happened then that the only societies capable of realizing this program are those who made a pact, yet not a pact of the contractual type in a sort of abstraction outside of time, but an historical pact. And for him, the western societies are the societies that gathered, firstly, the liberal forms of Christianity, and secondly, the inheritance of the Enlightenment, when this inheritance did not consider religion as an absolute enemy but as its 'other,' and thirdly – I shall insist above all – the inheritance of Romanticism that brought with it two things: a very lively feeling of the closeness between man and nature and the interiority of the heart. Where we find the balance between these three great forces – Judeo-Christianity, critical rationalism, and ecological emotivism – there is a possibility of a "reasonable discord," but one that becomes a founding value. I do not know if Lyotard is close to this position. I owe nothing to Lyotard, I do not know him well. It is quite possible that we say the same thing, but without consulting each other. I believe that he never quotes me and I never quote him; we live alongside each other. That's the way it is...[42]

Yvanka Raynova: I apologize, but when I was listening to you, I had the impression that there are some resemblances with postmodernism...

Paul Ricoeur: Please, do not speak to me about postmodernism, because it just infuriates me. And I'll tell you why: because I do not know what *is* modern. In my home town in Brittany, "modern" means to have a sewer system.

Yvanka Raynova: To have public sewers?

Paul Ricoeur: Yes, to have sewers, because there are none, and that means getting modernized.
[We laugh.]
But I do not want to make fun; I am set, for two reasons, against the notion of postmodernism. Firstly because I do not know what "modern" wants to say, and then because

---

[42] After I had disconnected my tape, I learned from Professor Ricoeur that the main reason of the distance between him and Lyotard is that, in 1968, Lyotard was among those who attacked him and who contributed to his resignation as Dean of the Faculty.

we do not know in what time we live. The darkness, the opaqueness of the present to itself seems to me completely fundamental. Now, with postmodernism, we are in a philosophy of history with the very hypothesis that there is no philosophy of history. I see there a contradiction, absolved by the historic qualification "postmodernism," just because it *is* a historic qualification; yet it is a definition in regard to a different period and thus the construction of a philosophy of history. I would say that this is the worst of all, because this is a philosophy of history that is made from a dark moment, opaque to itself. I do not know what the historians will say about us thirty years from now. I only want to refer to what people said in the fifties, because I am old enough to know. I still remember Emmanuel Mounier writing, yes *writing*: "There are only three living philosophies, Marxism, Existentialism and Personalism." And these three died, ha, ha... Speaking of current philosophies, what will still be living in ten years? I have no idea. There is nobody who can tell me, or tell Lyotard. That's just the way it is...

Yvanka Raynova: And nevertheless, when you said that you do not believe in a supranational point of view that would lead to a universal history, it seems that you join Rorty.[43] Especially since, for him and for you, utopia has a regulative function. Yet Rorty is considered as one of the representatives of postmodernism.[44]

Paul Ricoeur: Why not? We can take Rorty's ideas without using the word postmodernism. As far as I know, the word postmodernism had a very precise signification in architecture. We can thus think very well without using the word postmodernism. I am also very sensitive to Habermas' opinion, that the project of the Enlightenment is not yet exhausted. That means that modernity is not at an end.

Yvanka Raynova: Maybe there is no longer a philosophy of history, but there are still, today, historic narratives. To go back to my question, using the vocabulary of Lyotard,

---

[43] Richard Rorty, "Cosmopolitanism Without Emancipation: A Response to Jean-Francois Lyotard," in *Objectivity, Relativism and Truth. Philosophical Papers*, vol. 1 (Cambridge: Cambridge University Press, 1991), 211-220.

[44] Steven Best and Douglas Kellner, *Postmodern Theory* (New York: The Guildford Press, 1991), 1, 211, 263; Hans Bertens, *The Idea of the Postmodern. A History* (London; New York: Routledge, 1995), 138-159.

what type of narrative does hermeneutic phenomenology offer: a "grand" or a "small" narrative?

Paul Ricoeur: To begin with, not everything is a narrative. A narrative is a privileged shape of discourse having to do with time. As soon as we have to deal with the existence of people in time there is a problem with ordering all these histories in the time in which they occurred, i.e., the histories that people have written and that they have lived. A narrative has several levels, beginning with the little histories of everyday life, right up to the histories on the grand scale of Braudel, which covers the history of the (whole) Mediterranean. But I believe that what Lyotard called "*grand récits*" is something else altogether: it means grand constructions like socialism, staking out a claim to bring salvation. I believe that these have now been reduced to being utopias; but it is also necessary to keep 'utopia' as such.

Yvanka Raynova: During this seminar you have repeatedly mentioned Derrida. What are the crossing points between you and him, and what do you not share in his approach?

Paul Ricoeur: I like his first works on Husserl very much, *Speech and Phenomena* and then *Of Grammatology*. After that I followed his work rather less closely, especially all the parts on deconstruction, and I joined him once again in his recent work on the politics of friendship and the texts on justice, which places him again in the vicinity of Levinas. I believe that he develops a sort of grand curve close to Levinas, at least as an interpreter of Husserl, and that he then develops his own work aimed directly against the idea of metaphysics. This part did not interest me a great deal, because I have in no way the same idea of metaphysics. He considers it as a coherent attempt, derived from an ultra-dogmatic Platonism that opposes the intelligible and the sensitive, etc., and all that he calls "binary systems." Already his reading of Plato, that is ultimately that of Heidegger's, does not appear to me to correspond with two aspects of Platonism that escape this definition of "metaphysics." First there are these Platonic dialogues that end in absolutely nothing and that are an example of a thought in dialogue. It is the drama of the dialogue that is much more important, here, than the theory, and thus the reduction of Plato to Platonism seems to me very debatable. Next there are the later dialogues, beginning with *Sophist* and *Theatetus*, through *Philebus* and especially *Parmenides*, which have to do with an open ultra-dialectical construction that can even be considered as a type of criticism of classic Platonism. Thus classic Platonism is taken between a beginning and an end: The Socratic dialogues that are aporetic dialogues, and then the large dialectical constructions that are an open investigation of transcendental systems that cannot be reduced to the theory of ideas. Then, you see, it is a kind of doubting of the notion of metaphysics. I will continue by saying that I am much more worried about the multiplicity of systems of metaphysics than about the unity of metaphysics, because that is more important. In a sense it is more serious for us. Let us take for example the relation between Spinoza and Descartes. It is very difficult to say whether this is metaphysics. I cannot find there any metaphysical thought. I have the impression that it (the project of the deconstruction of metaphysics) is a construction destined only to be deconstructed. This means that I am much more interested in the approaches of reconstruction like the possibility of reopening a certain number of issues closed by the Greeks; I think for example of the polysemy of the verb that we find developed in Book E2 of *Metaphysics*, where Aristotle says that the notion of being means many different things like substance, true and false being, potential and actual being, etc. For my own work, I wondered if it were possible to conceptually reconstruct the bases of an anthropology that would have as a guideline the active person, thus constantly implementing categories like those of active being, potential being, actual being, etc. I discussed this reconstruction in the article that follows my *Intellectual Autobiography*.[45] It is a long article entitled "From metaphysics to morality," where I follow the long

---

[45] Paul Ricoeur, *Réflexion faite. Autobiographie intellectuelle* (Paris: Editions Esprit, Seuil, 1995). This Autobiography was first published in English as *Intellectual Autobiography of Paul Ricoeur*, in Lewis Edwin Hahn, ed., *The Philosophy of Paul Ricoeur* ("The Library of Living Philosophers", vol. 22, Chicago and La Salle, Illinois: Open Court, 1995), 1-53. The article of metaphysics (mentioned in the text hereafter) was published in 1994 on the occasion of the centenary of the journal *Revue de métaphysique et de morale*, by Ricoeur as its editor, and attached to the French edition of Ricoeur's Autobiography as "De la métaphysique à la morale," in idem, *Réflexion faite*, 83-115.

route since the meta-categories of Plato's *Parmenides* and Aristotle's *Metaphysics* through an anthropology of acting, where the notion of being is taken in the Aristotelian sense of act and potency. In the conference, which I gave here in Naples, I continued this line of thought by speaking about the capacity of the person and its opening on ethics, with a reconstruction of the idea of responsibility from the idea of imputability, i.e., the capacity of man to consider himself as the author of his own acts. You see, this is an approach of reconstruction that is one among others and that claims in no way to be able to cover the entire field; it takes place in a space of open controversy. It is at the end of this path that I encounter Derrida, because in his last works he was interested a great deal in the idea of justice, just as was Lyotard. In this way we meet, in a sort of "gang," with the idea of justice, in the neighborhood of Levinas. It is, if you like, a "redealing of the cards," after the cards were shuffled and, following a period of deconstruction which was also the structuralist period, they were dealt again... Here we have a long history which I covered in an extremely friendly relationship with Derrida. We have always kept in touch and have a good relationship. For example, after the death of Levinas, Derrida gave an admirable speech at his funeral, and I wrote to Derrida that I would have liked to have given this speech myself. He answered me with a very long and extremely friendly letter, ending with the assurance of his affectionate thoughts. We are in a very complex kind of relationship, between men who are very different and yet very close. All the time, when someone tries to oppose us, we both resist.

Yvanka Raynova: The notion of deconstruction provokes, in many philosophers, the same aversion as that of postmodernism. But is it not possible to see in deconstruction a crossing point between Derrida and yourself, since in different writings you stress the positive role of criticism?

Paul Ricoeur: Yes. But I am particularly close to the position taken by Gadamer in his discussions with Derrida. Because Gadamer was always very attentive to Derrida, and in fact he tries perhaps to bring the program of deconstruction to the deconstruction of the scholastic components of systemic thought. I will give you an example of where deconstruction seems to me completely justifiable. Spinoza presents his system as a geometrical demonstration with theorems, etc. But, to enter into the thought of Spinoza, it is really necessary to go beyond this demonstrative apparatus in order to find out what the dynamics of the system, or what he calls *actuosa substantia*, actually are, that is, God as essentially a generative power of the totality of being. There is a basic intuition, which is not transmitted by a geometrical construction. After all, Bergson argued this in his great text on intellectual intuition, where he says that every great philosopher said only one thing, but this thing was always masked by an apparatus of arguments so that we have to break through these in order to access its generative intuition. This is a positive way of conceiving the idea of deconstruction.

Yvanka Raynova: To touch the heart of this "generative intuition" of philosophy: is not the task of the philosopher as hermeneutician to be the intermediary between the Visible and the Invisible, *Sein* and *Sollen*, i.e., a critical consciousness reminding us of spiritual values such as justice...

Paul Ricoeur: What is your question now?

Yvanka Raynova: ...My question is whether this task of philosophy and hermeneutics does not get lost when we reduce it to the method of interpretation of narratives and texts? I ask you this question in view of your definition of hermeneutics as an interpretation of texts and metaphoric narratives and of what you just said on the living and generative aspects of philosophy. Is there not a sort of tension here? To formulate it in terms of a famous metaphor, is it not the letter that kills and the spirit "the one who gives life"? (John 6:63)

Paul Ricoeur: I would say that the task of philosophy is complex, multiple and even contradictory. As an educator, I will first say that we have the task of passing on an inheritance, that we should see to it that people still read Plato, Aristotle, Kant, etc. It is an important task, because it differs from the task of scientists. Scientists do not teach the history of sciences, they teach the science which is made. But *we* have an enormous past. Secondly, it is necessary to maintain – and I will add, also to restore – a dialogue with the sciences. What appears to me to be the weak point of philosophy since Hegel, is to have broken with the sciences. There are only a few exceptions. Bergson still had, to a certain extent, contact with biology, but in general, philosophy closed back in on itself in a kind of solipsism, especially since Nietzsche. The idea of the death of God became in fact the death of man, and the death of man, the death of philosophy. Since then we have not stopped asking whether or not philosophy died; I would say that the critique of metaphysics is part of this endless self-criticism. In opposition to this, I insist on the necessity of having a dialogue with one science or other – with mathematics, physics, biology, or the human sciences, like history and linguistics. Then there is the third task – and here I answer your question more directly – the task of mediation between everyday problems, but only on condition of having addressed the other two tasks. Concisely, the task of philosophy would be firstly to protect our inheritance, secondly, to enter into discussions with scientists, and thirdly, to enact what I call "practical wisdom," that is, the passage from norms to concrete situations. That is the reason why I am interested in judiciary problems such as laws, punishment, rehabilitation, that is to say, in problems of the intersection between the large institutional structures and the everyday practice of law – the breaking of laws, the establishing of guilt, etc. There is here another domain of the concrete, namely medical ethics, which has enormous influence, not only on the everyday life of the patient, but also on the experimental medicine of the researchers. Current researchers have enormous possibilities of genetic manipulation, of intervention in the human genome, and there is, for the first time, such a distance between what is possible and what is allowed; philosophers are therefore involved in this work. Another practical domain, next to the legal and the medical domain, is that of communication. Here we are confronted with the question of how to intervene in these incredible capacities opened by current communication. Following the advent of television there is today, along with the Internet, a sort of globalization of communication. I would open a bracket, here, to say that we tend to use the word 'globalization' only for the market, while in fact we have to deal with three globalizations: technological and economic globalization, and globalization of entertainment – we can say that the United States became the world supplier of international entertainment – and a type of world market of signs that nobody controls, except those who have access to the Internet networks. We now have the production of virtual images and communication without control – because we have no authority to control this open system. This is the third intersection point. I shall also raise a fourth, because I speak here about what interests me now; this is the understanding of our time by means of history, or the problem of the history of the twentieth century. And I am particularly interested in this problem, because it is in some way "my own" history. I mean that my memory actually goes back to the First World War. I was brought up by my grandfather who told me stories from his youth and who enabled me to know something of the history of the second half of the nineteenth century. I am also blessed with a good memory, and am confronted with a long history, which explains my interest in the work of the historians. Now, what is the commonality in all this:

my interests in the law, medical ethics, the world of communication and a knowledge of history? I would say two things. Firstly, that in all these domains we have to deal with a type of logic, a logic that is not formal, nor even a logic of proof, but essentially a logic of probability. I was greatly interested in the level of discourse that is located between the demonstrative and, let us say, the sophistic. The real problem is, not to slide into sophistry on the excuse that we cannot get any evidence. To hold to the level of an honest rhetoric, it is necessary to have a logic of probability. The second is the passage to concrete decision; because in all these domains we have to pass from the general, *lex*, to the particular, to judgments in concrete situations. It is this passage from a general law to the decision-in-situation through argumentations of probability before making the actual decision that is of interest. Then, in all the domains that I have indicated, there is a concrete decision-taking confronted with the solitude of judgment, but also with the practice of shared advice. All this is a "vast program," as General de Gaulle would say.

Yvanka Raynova: And what are, in your opinion, the lessons of the history of the twentieth century that the philosopher should retain?

Paul Ricoeur: Philosophers should not forget that history has multiple aspects and requires different approaches. All that I have just said on the shape of philosophical activity was put in interdisciplinary terms. The philosopher should help argumentation along with advice, always requiring correct arguments in the discussion. If you use the word freedom, what do you mean with that word? There is a deep agreement between what is called hermeneutic reason and analytical philosophy, namely that the philosopher is responsible for conceptual clarity and argumentative rigor. He has to help others to practice what Habermas calls the "ethics of the discussion." What does 'ethics of the discussion' mean? It is to be ready to give the best argument and to allow the other one to give their best argument; it is the justice of truth.

Yvanka Raynova: But not everything passes to us through speech. What about violence?

Paul Ricoeur: Because of what I said on 'difficult forgiveness,' it is necessary to undertake a critique of the idea of forgiveness, in order to reach a much more complex idea of a deep cure for the memory and its wounds. It is necessary, for that, to have a very detailed view of what history imposed, by way of wounds on our individual and collective memories, and to work at the level of the depth of these wounds. All consolations that fail to reach this level are vain and even deceitful.

Yvanka Raynova: But there are irreparable injustices. Dostoevsky and Camus insisted on the irreparable evil in history, of the bestialities that can in no way be excused or, if you like, forgiven. On the other hand, we can make a mistake and support a regime or a leader whom we perceive as just, but who turns out to be monstrous.

Paul Ricoeur: I also say, in my chapter on forgiveness, that it is also necessary to accept the insolvent debt. I agree that I am an insolvent person, a debtor. To want to arrive at a clear conscience is a great aim; but I very much like Luther's word: "*simul iustus et peccator.*"[46]

Yvanka Raynova: No, it is not a question of having a "clear conscience" – who could claim to have never "sinned"? But that is exactly why we should not judge too severely people who had to live through circumstances which we did not ourselves have to endure.

Paul Ricoeur: Yes, but I judge myself. At the beginning of the conversations that I published under the title *Critique and Conviction*, I passed a very austere judgment on my own political opinions. I do not want to leave it to others to accuse me by saying: "For a whole year, Ricoeur was a follower of Pétain (*pétiniste*)." Yes, for a year I was a follower of Pétain. Moreover, I was a pacifist at a time when one should not be. [Smiles.]

Yvanka Raynova: I understand, but I was thinking more of the debate about Heidegger's political convictions and of the responsibility of the philosopher in general.

---

[46] At once righteous and sinful.

Paul Ricoeur: I have never written a single line on Heidegger's guilt. If I sometimes wrote critically on Heidegger, it is in blaming him for having passed over the Jewish inheritance and for having preferred the Presocratics. That is all. I have never said anything else, and all that I did say was at the philosophical level. I wrote it in the collection of essays in the series *Cahiers de l'Herne*.[47] My contribution was very short, half a page. I said there that Heidegger chose Parmenides over and against the prophets of Israel, against the "hated." I try to hold both perspectives, making repeated efforts to do so, as indeed I made at the beginning of our conversation.

Yvanka Raynova: But how should one have acted at that time? Today my colleagues say so easy that Heidegger should have resisted, but I doubt whether, if they had been living in Nazi Germany, they would have been anything other than Nazis themselves, because they have never dared to protest against Jivkov's regime. It is easy to criticize ve-

---

[47] Michael Haar, ed., *Martin Heidegger*, Cahiers de l'Herne, no. 45 (Paris: Éditions de l'Herne, 1983).

hemently when there is no danger, but, in fact, there are few true heroes. We know that most of those who resisted Hitlerism died, and that deserves much more than simple admiration. Other philosophers left, but not everyone could leave.

Paul Ricoeur: I feel responsible for what, in my tradition, fed Anti-Semitism. There is a whole part of Christianity which is responsible, and in that I feel responsible too. I am not responsible for gas chambers, but I am responsible for having authorized theological arguments to encourage political Anti-Semitism. For that, I am responsible in an ongoing self-criticism concerning this involvement. Consequently, it is not others, but myself that I accuse.

But to return to your question, there is one exemplary figure, and it is Jaspers. And, moreover, my first book was on Jaspers. It is to him that I owe my first debt and not to Heidegger. That leaves me completely free to say that what was missing in Heidegger is what I found in Jaspers, i.e., moral and political judgment. We cannot imagine, even for a single moment, that Karl Jaspers makes a mistake regarding Hitler. It is not only that his wife was Jewish, because, after all, Heidegger had a little Jewish mistress... Now their correspondence, which is terrible, is to be published. I read it in English, because in France there is a blackout, and I found a letter where Heidegger says to Arendt: "I could not be an Anti-Semite because I loved you." And, something that has only just been discovered: Hannah Arendt supervised all American translations of Heidegger so that the transmission of his thought would remain exact. She well knew that he was a Nazi, only there was something in her, perhaps the heart of the woman, or I do not know what... It is all very complicated. From a philosophical point of view the question was, whether we should see, in *Sein und Zeit*, the sources of Nazism. But this question was raised because of his rectorial speech of 1934 and the rereading of *Sein und Zeit*, which therefore was rather a sort of retrospective reading. I always warn against retrospective readings. It is necessary to put somebody who did not know the sequence in context, and Heidegger is entitled to be protected against such anachronisms. We cannot impute to the Heidegger of 1927 a knowledge of what was going to become the Nazi party.

Yvanka Raynova: But later he made a mistake and the entire question is how to interpret this mistake.

Paul Ricoeur: Here I will quote Levinas. He was asked: "Why do you never stop speaking about Heidegger, when you do not want to go to Germany?" – because, you know, he never set foot in Germany. His reply was: "Even the Devil gives rise to thought."

3. Narrative Identity in Retrospection

Yvanka Raynova: Dear Professor Ricoeur, in a few months[48] you will celebrate your 90th birthday – an important event for you as well as for the international philosophical community. How do you feel and what are you thinking about when you reconsider the past?

Paul Ricoeur: I am impressed at first by the diversity of the philosophical landscapes that I traversed, and more widely, by the historical epochs. I grew up in the time of the First World War and in the memory of the death of my father, who was killed in this war. That is why I always felt congruent to a philosopher such as Jan Patočka who did not stop repeating that Europe committed suicide in 1914. The date of 1914 is somewhat forgotten nowadays because it was marked by the atrocities of the Second World War. But in fact it was in 1914 that Europe was involved in a bad destiny as the result of an incomprehensible fault. At that time there were different states with different governments as for example the tsarist regime of Russia or the parliamentary system of England. The fall of the great empires

---

[48] This Interview was realized on the 17th of October 2002 in Naples, four months before the 90th birthday of Paul Ricoeur.

was ending with the collapse of the whole of Europe and its colonies. The colonies were abandoned by the colonizers before they could attain a state of maturity and so they found themselves in an adventure of freedom for which they were not yet prepared for. I shall not say more about this period, which was for me personally a period of joyous childhood. I spent it at the side of my grandparents who granted me an incredible amount of freedom for reading. I was an intense reader. I did not play much, but I read a lot, which is something that I have stopped doing now. I also remember the period of my university studies which was rather classic, very normal but which passed quite fast. I was a good student, I became a young professor and everything was well when suddenly the Second World War broke out. After a short campaign, where it seems to me that I was rather ridiculous than heroic, I was captured and became a prisoner of war. The five years I spent in captivity were of great importance to me because they were years of intensive reading and study of the German philosophical tradition. This occupation had a double sense for me: on the one side to deepen my knowledge of German philosophy in which I had specialized in and on the other to protest in a certain sense against what surrounded me. The true Germans were not "outside" but "inside," in my books. This allowed me to preserve a respectful image of the German culture. But at the same time I must say that I underestimated at this time the gravity and monstrousness of the totalitarian system because as a prisoner of war I was in a sense protected in the camps. It was only several years afterward that I realized the magnitude of the monstrousness of the system, which was doubled by Bolshevism (but very different in its means). As a matter of fact we removed the traces of this hideous period only with the fall of the Berlin Wall. Now we see that it was a long period, from 1945 till 1989, a period of the confrontation of the West with Communism and maybe – what I had not perceived at the beginning – with the wounds of the Second World War, in particular with the destruction of the Jewish people. That is the political background, in the widest sense of the word "political," or the type of political civilization in which I grew up in.

Speaking about the epochs of philosophic thought, I shall remind very quickly that after 1945, in the 1950s till 1970, philosophy was dominated by the confrontation with Existentialism under its shape mainly of Sartre and then with Marxism which was intellectually very active, notably in Italy and in France, but in no way in the Anglo-Saxon countries. There was also a polemical touch in the philosophic situation because of a basic disparity between a perfectly individualistic thought with that of Existentialism, and a thought associated with Marxism. I remember very well that my Marxist friends always lived in the fear of not thinking and acting according to the party line. There was thus a sort of hindrance to free thought.

Yvanka Raynova: Who is it that you have in sight when you say "Marxist friends"?

Paul Ricoeur: I am thinking here of many professional fields which were dominated by Marxism: even the French linguistics, a large part of the historical sciences, and almost the entire field of geography. In human sciences there was a very active presence of Marxism. They were very often rebel Marxists, but nevertheless Marxists. For them the end of the Soviet Union was a personal tragedy, which I respect a lot. At least it was in this frame that it was necessary to search for orientation. For my part, I was very strongly affected on the one hand by the Phenomenology of Edmund Husserl and on the other hand by the Personalism of Gabriel Marcel, Emmanuel Mounier and the journal *Esprit* which remained for me a place of intellectual filiation. It is on this double and polemical bottom – in the heart of Husserlian Phenomenology, which is a sort of Rationalism, and the cordiality of Personalism – that I tried to settle my own thought and to find my own approach. I was assisted by the discovery in the 1970s of the book by Hans-Georg Gadamer *Wahrheit und Methode*, which gave me a sort of third reference, a third position between Phenomenology and Personalism. I had a great friendship with Gadamer, a friendship moreover that was often critical. For example I did not agree with his interpretation setting truth against method. I shall say that I was prevented from writing about this opposition because of my discovery and occupation with the Anglo-Saxon thought, in particular the Analytical Philosophy; I taught in the United States where I was practically every year since 1954 and especially from 1970 when I began to teach at the University of Chicago. Then, confronted with the very rigorous, very argumentative thought of the Analytical Philosophy, I had as a Phenomenology insider to resist against a sort of anti-rational drive that emerged from European Phenomenology, mainly German and French. Thus, after this negotiation of my youth between Phenomenology and Personalism, I was involved in a sort of second negotiation between Hermeneutics, which is the theory of interpretation, mainly of texts, but also of thoughts, and analysis – the semiotic analysis, linguistic analysis, abstract analysis, and analysis of arguments. It is this middle road which I followed.

Yvanka Raynova: When we discuss your philosophical work so rich in "negotiations" it seems that you prefer that we speak rather about the evolution of the questions it poses than about its unity. Now the question about the human being as Subject and Self seems to form the center around which all other questions are grouped. This is exactly because you establish a connection between the question of the speaking Subject and the question of the acting and suffering Subject that we are directly confronted with such practical and axiological problems as in the Evil, the Fault, the Just and the Unjust. Could we consider, in this sense, your work as a hermeneutic Phenomenology of the Self?

Paul Ricoeur: The confrontation with the concrete problems of the historical and the personal Evil – problems of Justice as Plato would have said, as for him, this sphere covers the personal and the public – lead me to arrange many of my works together that were scattered around a guiding concept, which was the concept of *l'homme capable*, the capable man. I owe this focus on this center of gravity to one of my recent commentators and friends, Jean Greisch, who has just written a book on my philosophy – *L'itinérance du sens*.[49] In this book there is a very long chapter, which he calls *l'herméneutique de l'homme capable*.[50] This notion is completely convenient for me because parting from the concept of the acting and suffering man, as you just noticed, I added to it a third term, exactly that of

---

[49] Jean Greisch, *Paul Ricœur, l'itinéraire du sens* (Paris: Jérôme Millon, 2001).
[50] More exactly Greisch speaks not about a "hermeneutics of the capable man" but about a "phenomenology of the capable man" related to the "hermeneutics of the self" (ibid., 285 ff.).

the capable man. It poses the question of what man can do and of what he cannot. What he *can* do is precisely what became the center around which the questions of my later work were based upon. Personally I had not associated this expression with this unifying capacity. Greisch, who examines the whole of my work, begins with *L'homme faillible*,[51] one of my first books, published in 1950 – you see, already one half a century ago; I posed the question therein about the fragility of man in his capacities to think, act and feel. The notion of fragility exactly announced the development, of which I later lost sight of when I was confronted with the problems of linguistics, semiotics, and the very technical problems of language. But even inside the philosophy of language I again faced this notion because it was not only the logical structures of the language that interested me, but also the commitment of the speaking subject. The speaking subject is a subject which can do something, which can say, which can communicate with other people, which can converse. Then you see, the idea of

---

[51] Paul Ricœur, *L'homme faillible. Finitude et culpabilité I* (Paris: Aubier, Montaigne, 1960) [English: *Fallible Man*. Translated by Charles A. Kelbley (Chicago: Henry Regnery, 1965)].

"what we can" allows me to group together my contribution to the philosophy of language and the commitment of the speaking subject and also my interest for the agent of human action, who can act with and against others and who is consequently related to the structures of power, of order and violence.

But there is also the question about the faculty of narration, because a large part of my work was about the narrative. The third volume of *Temps et récit* ends moreover by a sort of retrospective glance. I introduced therein the idea of narrative identity,[52] the idea that we recognize ourselves in the capacity of narration. And finally it is what you are asking me to do now: you are asking me to perform an exercise of narrative identity.

[Laughter]

Yvanka Raynova: Your philosophy of the capable man is doubtlessly a "philosophy of man," but is it a sort of anthropology and, if yes, how can one interpret it in the con-

---

[52] Paul Ricœur, *Temps et récit*, tome III, 439-448 (English: *Time and Narrative*, vol. 3, 241-250).

text of phenomenology? As we know, Husserl and Heidegger emphasized repeatedly that it would be a grave error to interpret their thought in an anthropological sense.[53] On the other hand, Scheler and Sartre connected, although in a different way, the phenomenological method to philosophical anthropology.[54] Which side would you choose in this subject?

Paul Ricoeur: The word anthropology is problematic because it is employed in a very different way in human biology and in ethology, the sciences of the behavior. There is thus a physical and biologic anthropology, and a very material anthropology which is the study of the human brain. I used the word in the sense of philosophical anthropology to say exactly what man (l'homme) is and how he understands

---

[53] See Edmund Husserl, *Nachwort zu meinen "Ideen"* (Sonderdruck Halle: Max Niemeyer, 1930), 551; Martin Heidegger, *Sein und Zeit* (Tübingen: Max Niemeyer, 1993), 16-17, 48-50; de idem, *Über den Humanismus* (Frankfurt a. M.: Vittorio Klostermann, 1949), 21, 28; de idem, "Die Zeit des Weltbildes," in idem, *Holzwege* (Frankfurt a. M.: Vittorio Klostermann, 1950), 93, 99-100, 111-112.
[54] See Max Scheler, *Die Stellung des Menschen im Kosmos* (Darmstadt: Otto Reichl, 1928), 14 ff; Jean-Paul Sartre, *Situations IX* (Paris: Gallimard), 1972, 83.

himself as a human being (homme).[55] But I think that we should go back to Aristotle, because at the beginning of the *Nicomachean Ethics* he asks the following: in various professions there is a purpose and even a sort of perfection to be reached, but for the human being (homme) as a human (homme), is there a task, an *ergon*? Is there an assignment that is for the human being (homme) that is for example music for the musician or what is medicine for the doctor? What a "good doctor" is can be defined by the art of the doctor, what a "good musician" is could also be defined by art. But is there a goodness which would distinguish as a matter of fact the task to be a human being (homme)? This task was traditionally named happiness. Thus I remain very gladly in the horizon of this first Aristotelian question: is there an appropriate human assignment? This is a question about the way of reaching success, fulfillment and completion, and that is what we popularly call happiness. I do not hesitate, as my colleague Joachim Ritter, to make a jump

---

[55] Ricoeur employs the notion of "homme" (man) most of the time in the sense of the human being (être humain). I used both translations by employing "human being" in cases where it was necessary to emphasize the meanings of "humanitas" and "anthropos".

from Aristotle to Hegel. Because my interpretation of the principles of the philosophy of right, as structures helping the institutionalization of freedom, shows that they are completely comparable to Aristotle's search for what he designates as virtues or, in other words, the excellences which indicate the route of the human task in the direction of happiness. It is difficult to follow this route all the way to the end, which for Hegel leads towards the total, the absolute knowledge, but we can accompany him at least until the middle of the route, until that point of what I have just called institutionalization or institutions of freedom. It is the concept of the institution which chiefly interests me because I can see a way there of structuring the capable man at the level of his participation in the collective activity of our communities. We are capable of entering into symbolic systems, into normative systems and to speak very widely, in the most powerful sense of the word, into institutions.

Yvanka Raynova: We discover already in your first books, especially in the three volumes of *La philosophie de la volonté*, the problems of evil and suffering. I wonder if they do not lead to a previous, vaster question, that about the Just and the Unjust. You mentioned at the beginning of our conversation your father. In the impressive biographical work *Paul Ricoeur, les senses d'une vie*[56] François Dosse asserts that the death of your father, killed in the First World War, led you to put into question war and death. Is this the key to your personal and also philosophical interest in the problems of right and politics?

Paul Ricoeur: [Brief silence]. An outside observer such as Dosse, or Jean Greisch, who is also a friend of mine, can analyze my motives. But I am not capable of doing this. To do this means to make a sort of wild psychoanalysis of myself. For example a psychoanalyst friend said to me that what is important to me, maybe more than the death of my father is not only the additional death of my mother, but the total absence of the history of my mother, which was concealed in my paternal family. I remember that I had said: "The page of my mother is a blank page." And the psycho-

---

[56] François Dosse, *Paul Ricœur, les sens d'une vie* (Paris: La Découverte, 2000).

analyst answered: "But you never stop to cover this blank page with writing."

I do not know the worth of this wild psychoanalysis, which is not the result of a psychoanalytical cure. I am not the master of my deep motives, we do not know ourselves. But what I can speak about are the questions which I posed and explored. Because asking questions is to pursue an intellectual responsibility. Philosophy begins with questions, with texts and authors. I am responsible for having entered a field of problems or questions stated by philosophers, but I am not responsible for the motivations of my childhood.

Yvanka Raynova: In that case I do not know if it makes any sense to ask you if this blank page which symbolizes the absence of your mother can be put in touch with the blank page or the absence of problematization of the gender question and the problems of sex/gender differences. You wrote much about power, recognition, and just and unjust institutions – questions, which are connected to the problems of gender and the patriarchal structures that continue to contribute to social asymmetries, to the refusal of recognition and the politics of dominance. How should we explain this absence of the gender question in your work, a question, which is not only an object of feminist studies, but also of interest for the philosophy of "man" (philosophie de "l'homme") and for political theory?

Paul Ricoeur: As for my motives, I do not know them. But we can speak about my philosophical interest. I can say that I found that, for me, I was rather satisfied concerning this problem in Mrs. Héritier's work on the masculine/feminine.[57] I feel perfectly comfortable in this idea that the human being is originally a double, masculine-feminine, and I even resist certain psychoanalytical orientations, which actually would offer the symbol of the phallus a sort of supremacy onto the duality. I believe that there are at once two. You would say that there is not much about in my work. There is all the same, a text for which I have a large affection for…

---

[57] Cf. Françoise Héritier, *Masculin/Féminin. La pensée de la différence* (Paris: Odile Jacob, 1996) and *Masculin/Féminin II : Dissoudre la hiérarchie* (Paris: Odile Jacob, 2002).

Yvanka Raynova: Your essay in the volume on *Sexuality*?[58]

Paul Ricoeur: No, I am thinking of another text, despite the fact that the volume on sexuality anticipated the crisis of modern sexuality arising in the years 1965-1967. I am thinking here rather on my comment of the *Song of Songs* published in the book *Penser la Bible*,[59] which just appeared in Italian translation.[60] There I show an enthusiasm and a sort of deep tenderness. You should not judge me on this plan by what I have or have not written, because there also is the side of what I have lived and what I still shall live. I have never been in a debate with a women's or antifeminist movement, but I found enormous intellectual satisfaction in the book of Sylviane Agacinsky – the wife of

---

[58] Paul Ricœur, "La sexualité. La merveille, l'errance, l'énigme" [suivie de la présentation par Paul Ricœur des réponses aux enquêtes], in *Esprit* 28 (*La sexualité*), No. 11 (novembre 1960), 1665-1676 [English: "The Dimensions of Sexuality. Wonder, Eroticism and Enigma," in *Cross Currents* (Sexuality and the Modern World) 14, No. 2 (Spring 1964), 133-141].
[59] André LaCocque, Paul Ricœur, *Penser la Bible* (Paris: Seuil), 1998 [English: *Thinking Biblically: Exegetical and Hermeneutical Studies* (Chicago: University of Chicago Press, 1998)].
[60] André LaCocque, Paul Ricœur, *Come pensa la Bibbia: studi esegetici ed ermeneutica*. Edizione italiana a cura di Franco Bassani (Brescia: Paideia, 2002).

Lionel Jospin – who states a large plea for both, the feminine and the masculine.[61] The problems which I discuss do not appear to fundamentally distinguish between men and women. Let us take for example my last book *La mémoire, l'histoire, l'oubli.* I do not see where the gender question could be put there. I have never heard about a theory of feminine memory. The capacity of memories, recollections, reminiscences, the capacity to designate ourselves as a self, who remembers something, the problem of collective memory, the connection between history and memory – all these are problems that do not distinguish between men and women. It seems that I raised problems which could be designated as "unisex."

[Laughter]

Yvanka Raynova: What place does your treatise *The Right to Punish* (*Le droit de punir*) hold in the evolution of the questions which you are preoccupied with? Is it a more advanced elaboration of the Just or is it rather a complementary ethical study?

---

[61] Sylviane Agacinsky, *Politique des Sexes*. Précédé par *Mise au point sur la mixité* (Paris: Seuil, 2001).

Paul Ricoeur: It is at least an integral part of the problem of the Just. The court is in the city, but the prison is rarely in the city – it is forgotten by the citizens – and the failure not to be capable of protecting the safety of the citizens without punishing and without exercising this major punishment which is the deprivation of liberty, it is a large failure of society. My personal interest was to know if it was not also a large failure of philosophical thought, especially of moral thought. Because the texts on the right to punish, which I examine show the greatest philosophers in trouble. I wanted also to place the great philosophers in the situation of failure in regard to a fact which I consider to be an intellectual scandal, namely the fact that in order to compensate for the victims suffering we make the offender suffer and consequently we add suffering to the suffering. I called that an intellectual scandal by taking the word scandal nearly in a literal meaning of the word, that is in the meaning of embarrassment, of a stumbling block. I believe that it is very important to show philosophy not always as successful, nor even only in deliberation, but also in a situation of failure.

Yvanka Raynova: In 1911 the Austrian philosopher Oskar Kraus, a follower of Brentano, published a book on the same subject – *Das Recht zu strafen*.[62] He begins as you did with the theory of Plato and redraws the problem of punishment through the whole history of philosophy and the theory of right until present-time. But contrary to you he opts – and it is a classic thesis – for a proportional punishment of the fault: "The guiltier should be punished harsher than the less guilty" ("Der Schuldigere soll schärfer büssen, als der minder Schuldigere").[63] In his argumentation he refers to the ethics of Brentano according to which we can distinguish in an evident way between right and false judgments. What would you object to this approach and is there something that we could actually use from Brentano's conception on which the first Husserlian ethics bases on?

Paul Ricoeur: I do not know that Husserl expressed himself concerning this question.

---

[62] Oskar Kraus, *Das Recht zu strafen* (Stuttgart: Ferdinand Enke, 1911).
[63] Ibid., 79, 86, 135 ff.

Yvanka Raynova: I have in mind his ethics lectures of 1908-1914,[64] where he reproduced the schema of Brentano's practical philosophy.

Paul Ricoeur: This does not surprise me ...

I have no fundamental objections against the idea to proportion punishments to the offences; it is at the bottom of penal theory. However, this proposition treats the question of "how" and not "why" to punish. It is in the "why" that I see philosophical trouble. Because all philosophers who emphasized language and reason were suddenly confronted with the body. What is what suffers? It is the body. And thus there is a very deep difficulty of rationalist philosophies. Those who made a semiotics of passions are always searching for the sense, the meaning, without examining affliction and suffering. We can say that the punishment "casts" the suffering to the attention of the philosopher because it confronts him with the definition of punishment which consists in making one suffer the unjust justly. But in

---

[64] See Edmund Husserl, *Vorlesungen über Ethik und Wertlehre 1908-1914* (*Husserliana*, Bd. XXVIII, Dordrecht: Kluwer, 1988).

the expression "to suffer justly" there seems to be a sort of enmity of words which makes it to where "justly" appeals to our reason but "to suffer" refers to human pain. The acting and suffering man is suffering in a radical way because of an injustice that he committed or that he has to endure by being punished.

Yvanka Raynova: But can we make such a disjunction between the body and the psyche? Is it only the body which suffers? Every physical suffering is also a psychical one.

Paul Ricoeur: Certainly. The deprivation of liberties envelops a whole range of sufferings beginning with the deprivation of social relations which is a deep infringement on language. There are prisoners which spend weeks and maybe years in solitude without speaking with anybody. And thus the thought confined in silence is a sickening thought.

I do not mean that we have to necessarily content ourselves with these results. In particular in the last lesson of my seminar on punishment I am going to examine several attempts to humanize pain and prepare the punished for rehabilitation. I did not pay special attention to the regulations in France, but I noticed that here, in Italy, the word rehabilitation figures in the constitution as the meaning of punishment. Thus there is a sort of rationalization, if you want, of a society which says: "I punish, I cause suffering, but it is only done so in order to rehabilitate, to discharge." Consequently, if we claim that this is the purpose of punishment, it is necessary to attest this concretely by reforming prisons. I also think that before prison and before court it is rather necessary to develop the procedures of conciliation and compensation. In fact the project to avoid the court becomes very difficult at present because we are in a period of regression due to the extension of insecurity. We are confronted with increasing insecurity not simply by terrorism and already known acts such as criminality but also by the regression of the inhibitions, of the brakes in the advanced democratic societies. I do not think that human desires are more violent today than they were in the past. But they were maybe better controlled not just by institutions, but also by the precocious interiorization of norms during the childhood. There is something which does not work any more. It is the deep embarrassment which creates the problem of punishment in which is overflowed by the problem of the social treatment of insecurity and the anarchical motivations, in particular the motivations of adolescence. Our societies are confronted with the necessity to educate before punishing, because often we punish where we did not manage to educate. We are obliged to stimulate education and to confront it with repression.

All this is very difficult to assume intellectually because philosophers try to be something what Hegel called "beautiful souls." How can one be resigned to be a "beautiful soul"? One of the first human rights registered in the constitution is the right of security. This is originally not a repressive concept, but a principle of freedom: we are not free if we are not safe, if there is a lack of security in our habitation, in our environment, in our city. Thus the problems of security are real problems.

Yvanka Raynova: Your treatise on the right to punish is topical in regard to the attacks of September 11th and the measures of punishment or vengeance taken thereafter.

What is your position towards the current politics of the United States, especially their war against terrorism and Iraq?

Paul Ricoeur: At first there is a disproportion in power. We are at present in a situation where we have a single superpower, which can do everything alone. Thus it does not ask for our assistance, but for our compliance. It is a very difficult situation, because there are two inextricably involved realities. At first, there is effectively a new phenomenon, namely a new sort of terrorism which is not any more exercised by a power, but by an unattainable clandestine group. The fact that the day before yesterday Australian young people were massacred in a discotheque in Bali is a real fact which shows that because of this new form of the terrorism, there is no longer security anywhere. Secondly, there is the imperial politics of a single superpower which is able to exercise force. Our role is, in my opinion, to defend at the utmost the international institutions. They are fragile, but they are our only recourse against the hubris of a superpower, which is in charge of defending us against this new form of terrorism, but which simultaneously pursues its own imperial goals. It is very difficult to gain orientation in this new situation and to find a balance between on the one hand, the necessity to chase after the root of terrorism, and on the other hand to exercise justice towards the poorest, towards those who are crushed by history as for example the Palestinians.

Yvanka Raynova: What are the imperative prerequisites in order to arrive at a more just world in the current situation?

Paul Ricoeur: It is necessary to begin at first with our own nation. We have just raised a global problem: the problem of security in the contemporary world. But one of the roots of this problem consists in the following: only the market economy creates wealth – it is a fundamental fact that after the defeat of the Bolshevik totalitarian society, the market economy is the only option –, but how to face the paradox that the system which is alone to create wealth produces at the same time the most disparities? Our hesitating, staggering politics – no matter if they are oriented on the right or left– have to resolve the same enigma: how to take advantage of the productive capacity of the market economy and to correct the injustices and disparities which increase with this production of wealth? This problem is like the quadrature of the circle. Our regimes are confronted with a contradiction – I do not assert a fundamental difference between the right and the left at this point – because it is difficult to have both at the same time, namely to produce wealth and to limit disparities. Nevertheless, that is what we have to do now.

Yvanka Raynova: When you opt for a non-violent justice in punishment, what kind of justice do you envisage then for the victims? There are extreme cases where the victim remains a victim, remains *différend*, and moreover where it is just impossible to repair injustice, because even if the criminal is severely punished this will not return the life of the killed, nor the original psycho-physical condition of the violated child or of the violated woman. In such cases, when the tribunal centers the concern of justice on the criminal by trying to ease his/her punishment then the injustice done to the victim seems to increase.

Paul Ricoeur: The non-violent justice has no claim to answer the question about the irreparable. You evoked the departed who will not return to life; in that case there is no violent or non-violent justice, but something irreparable. I will remind one of a few reflections that I made on another concern, namely on the place of mourning, which can be applied here. I made a long analysis on the relation between memory and mourning by examining Freud's essay *Mourning and Melancholy*.[65] As I noticed in a chapter of *La mémoire, l'histoire, l'oubli* there is no work of memory without a work of mourning.[66] I insist on the notion of work and on the expression "work of mourning," which sounds extremely powerful in German: *Trauerarbeit*. Mourning is work and nobody can circumvent this work, which is related to the irreparable, to the implacable, and maybe also to the inscrutable. We cannot clarify everything. There is

---

[65] See Sigmund Freud, *Trauer und Melancholie* (in *Gesammelte Werke*, Bd. X. Frankfurt am Main: Fischer, 1915); English: "Mourning and Melancholy," (in Sigmund Freud, *Collected Papers*, vol. 4. Translated by Joan Riviere. New York: Basic Books, 1959).
[66] See Paul Ricœur, *La mémoire, l'histoire, l'oubli* (Paris: Seuil, Collection Essais, 2000), 86-89, 92-97, 468-470.

an ideology of transparency which seems to me to be pretentious.

Yvanka Raynova: All right. But if we take into account the relation between violence and recognition then this raises the question of how could a *différend* pass from a level of total exclusion to the level of recognition where discourse and dispute become possible? Can he/she attain this level without using any violence? There is a *fight* for recognition which cannot always escape from violence…

Paul Ricoeur: At least the procedure of non-violent justice cannot be improvised, it needs much preparation. I would like to remind one here of an experiment that I studied very closely, namely that of South Africa's "Truth and Reconciliation Commission." An immense preliminary work of the archbishop Tutu and of Nelson Mandela[67] was needed in order to form not just a tribunal, but also a public author-

---

[67] In 1995 President Nelson Mandela appointed Archbishop Tutu to chair South Africa's "Truth and Reconciliation Commission," the body was set up to probe gross human rights violations between 1960 and the President's inauguration in 1994. Archbishop Tutu presented the Commission's Report to the President in October 1998. See Desmond Tutu, *No Future without Forgiveness* (New York: Doubleday, 1999).

ity of confrontation. This requires much physical safety and the assurance that what is said will not be used for incrimination and accusation. Thus it supposes not only careful preparations, but also guarantees what is very rarely given. Also a certain historical epoch has to be finished in order to clarify: it is only after the end of the apartheid in South Africa that the coming to power of the black majority was made institutionally possible concerning the treatment of "non-violent justice," of public confrontation where the double narrative became possible, and even protected and welcomed. It is thus a way to limit the place of the tribunal with its procedures of charge, judgment and punishment. But it is a rare experience and its circumstances are historically very precise: they form a sort of armistice in the violence. This means that there must be a favorable background. Such a background is actually lacking in the situation of the Palestinians and the Israelis, although I think that it should materialize in the future. But now we do not see the conditions.

Yvanka Raynova: What are these conditions? Do you believe for example in the possibility of forming a world court where certain conflicts could be resolved?

Paul Ricoeur: Yes, this possibility exists since the United Nations founded the International Court of Justice. But this one can work only after ratification by an important majority of governments. We know that for example the United States refused in advance to allow their military personnel to appear in such a court. Thus there is enormous work to be done so that this penal work really becomes truly universal, that is to say to have the competence for all offences of all powers and all members of any armed powers. At present we have three courts, which work: the court of Rwanda and two courts treating the affairs of Milosevic, of Bosnia and of Kosovo. Thus we cannot truly state that international law does not work.

Yvanka Raynova: What will the duty of Europe be in this field?

Ricoeur: In the first place it is to begin to exist collectively, institutionally. We entered now into a process of extension which is going faster than the process of structuralization. This delay can be very expensive because we risk building simply a space of free exchange of Anglo-Saxon types instead of Western European. That is why I have a very deep admiration for the suggestions of the German Foreign Minister Joschka Fischer, who seems to me to be at present the only credible visionary.

Yvanka Raynova: The problems of justice and recognition, which we just approached, refer at least to social relations. The dialectics between the "short" and the "long" relations is to find in your first writings as well as in your more recent work where you substitute the dialectics between the "*socius*" and the "fellow man," elaborated in *History and truth* (1955), with that of the "friend" and the "each," developed in *The Self as Another* (1990). In this way the place of charity is taken by that of friendship. But can friendship replace the virtue of charity, which is not a relation of exchange or of reciprocity, but a completely disinterested action steered even towards strangers? Why do you not use the notion of charity any more?

Paul Ricoeur: I tend to ask the inverse question: can charity substitute for justice? I do not believe so. Compassion introduces some friendship into power relations, the relations of exercise and the limitation of power. Justice has the obligation to give to each their own and to measure it. I will refer here very quickly to a great work that I admire a lot, namely to John Rawls' *Theory of Justice*. The principle of this theory involves in no way compassion or charity but calculation, a calculation which expresses the moral rationality by saying that it is necessary to compensate for the increase of the privilege of the most endowed with the decrease of the disadvantage of the most discriminated. It is there that a sort of dialectic of compensation which is the object of calculation. Charity brings in our interpersonal relations this element of tenderness, sympathy and sharing the suffering, which quells violence and justice, than by fighting against injustice, justice becomes violent. It is here that I refer to a recent discovery that I made in my readings, that is to say Aristotle had widened his concept of *filia* to the political domain with an argument which exactly interests us now: the fact that the social link bases not only on confrontation, not even on the internal danger and the protection against the "outside" that he called a revolt, but in the will to live happily together. To want to be happy together is the basic idea of what he called "political friendship." Thus I shall attempt to make a link between charity, which is an exchange of compassion between one person and another, and an element of sweetness and tenderness in our social relations which makes it to where the other becomes a life companion and not an opponent.

Yvanka Raynova: But in *The Self as Another* you do not speak anymore about charity, you speak about friendship. All right, friendship is, like charity, an interpersonal relationship, nevertheless it is based on reciprocity, whereas charity is an unreciprocated, disinterested action. That is why friendship cannot replace charity.

Paul Ricoeur: You quote *The Self as Another*, but my last book *La mémoire, l'histoire, l'oubli* ends with a long epilogue about forgiveness.[68] I developed a whole analysis of forgiveness where I give satisfaction to your question.

Yvanka Raynova: I quote *The Self as Another* because it is there that you elaborated your "small ethics."

Paul Ricoeur: Exactly. I was not satisfied and that is why I added this epilogue on forgiveness of which it is not a question in "small ethics." I would simply say that I did not neglect this problem and that I go very far even in the political projections of forgiveness under the shape of the reduction of punishment, the sweetening of the prisoner's situation, and of the non-institutional charitable activity by diverse non-profit associations. I think that the public activity of justice must be accompanied by free, voluntary and charitable activities.

Yvanka Raynova: By making reference to Hanna Arendt you noticed in a text[69] that it is through stories that the sub-

---

[68] Paul Ricœur, "Le pardon difficile," in idem, *La mémoire, l'histoire, l'oubli*, 593-656 (English: *Memory, History, Forgetting*, 457-506). See also Domenico Jervolino, *Ricoeur. L'amore difficile* (Roma: Edizioni Studium, 1995).

[69] Paul Ricœur, "Préface à *Condition de l'homme moderne*," in idem,

ject, the "who" of the action can express himself. But can we always speak about everything, tell everything? Let us take once again, for example, the act of suffering and pain. There are many cases when a violated woman or a violated child does not manage to tell what took place effectively, because she/he is disturbed, traumatized, or because she/he feels shameful. Then how to find out the dimension of the committed evil or the pain imposed to the victim? In other words, if we put the story, the narrative in the center, can we be sure that it will really describe what occurred and all that which takes place in the human soul?

Paul Ricoeur: I do not believe so. Permit me to refer once again to my last work, because I made there lengthy analyses on testimony, especially on impossible testimony. We met this problem in other circumstances other than those that you evoked, speaking of violated children, in particular in the face of the pedophilia, which is a redoubtable drama and a contemporary social disaster. I am thinking here rather on the survivors of the Shoah whose experience is

---

Lectures I. Autour du politique (Paris: Seuil, 1991), 60-61.

the object of the book of Primo Levi *Si c'était un homme*[70] and on his other essay[71] on the survivors which precisely demonstrates the impossibility to speak, to say. It is true that there is an internal limit of the capacity to narrate, but there is also a very positive aspect in regard to certain possibilities, which is indeed the secret. You speak here about a hindrance, but there is also a concern in not telling everything in order to keep the secret of intimacy. I reject a tendency of our contemporary society and literature which is the tendency of transparency, to tell everything and to go to the limit of scandal in the name of the freedom of expression. We touch here a will of transgressing a very positive value which is not the publicly sharing character of the personal story or the story of a couple of intimacy. I shall say that everything cannot and must not be put in the public space. We are for a period of provocation to tell everything, a practice that legitimates itself by the value of transparency. But I shall say that there is also value in the

---

[70] Primo Levi, *Si c'était un homme* (Paris: Pocket, 1988); See also Tzvetan Todorov, *Face à l'extrême* (Paris: Seuil, 1994), 270-271.
[71] Primo Levi, *La Trêve* (Paris: Grasset, 1997); de idem, *Les naufragés et les rescapés: 40 ans après Auschwitz* (Paris: Gallimard, 1989).

clear-obscure to be protected. This value demands for one to not want to know everything, to not want to tell everything, but to accept the clear-obscure in our relations to ourselves and to the others.

Yvanka Raynova: I respect this value and I will take it as a sign to end my questions. Thank you very much for the conversation and especially for bringing clarity to your positions without removing their discreet charm of obscurity.

Paul Ricoeur:
A chronology with biographical sources

- Born 27th February 1913 in Valence (France); his mother dies six months later
- 1915 – his father, an English professor, is killed at the military front; Ricoeur and his sister are consigned to their paternal grandparents and an aunt, and both move to Rennes
- 1929-1930 – Ricoeur completes his high school studies under the care of his philosophy professor, Roland Dalbiez
- 1930-1933 – studies at Rennes University, where in 1993 he obtains his philosophy degree
- 1934 – writes his Masters thesis on reflexive philosophy: *Le problème de Dieu chez Lachelier et de Lagneau* (*The Problem of God in the Work of Lachelier and Lagneau*); moves to the Sorbonne and participates at the Gabriel Marcel's "Friday meetings," where he encounters the phenomenology of Husserl
- 1935 – obtains the philosophy aggregation at the Sorbonne, and finished second-best his class; marries childhood friend, Simone Lejas; then teaches at Colmar in Alsace
- 1936-1939 – learns German and pursues studies of Husserl and Heidegger (*Sein und Zeit*); writes several pacifist articles, which he will designate later as fallacious/deceptive/misleading?
- 1937 – his first son, Jean-Paul, is born
- 1938 – his second son, Marc, is born
- 1939-1945 – resides in Germany: in August 1939, Ricoeur takes a German course at Munich University, to improve his language skills; in September, World War II begins and he is mobilized by the French army; in 1940,

Ricoeur is captivated in Dormans; during his years in capture he reads Karl Jaspers and in 1943 begins the translation of the first volume of Husserl's *Ideen*

- 1945-1948 – teaches at the Cévenol College in Chambon-sur-Lignon; at the same time becomes a research fellow at the National Center for Scientific Research (CNRS) in Paris and continues to widen further his phenomenological studies
- 1947 – his first book is published: *Karl Jaspers et la philosophie de l'existence* (Paris: Seuil), written with Michel Dufrenne
- 1948 – succeeds Jean Hyppolite on his history of philosophy chair at Strasbourg University, where he lectures until 1957; publishes *Gabriel Marcel et Karl Jaspers. Philosophie du mystère et philosophie du paradoxe* (Paris: Temps Présent)
- 1950 – endorses his doctoral thesis about the phenomenology of the will published under the title *Le volontaire et l'involontaire* (first volume of *Philosophie de la volonté*); Gallimard publishes his French translation of Husserl's *Ideen I*
- 1955 – publication of *Histoire et vérité* (Paris: Seuil)
- 1957 – becomes professor of general philosophy at the Paris–Sorbonne University, where he teaches until 1967
- 1960 – publication of the next two volumes of *Philosophie de la volonté – Finitude et culpabilité I: L'homme faillible* and *Finitude et culpabilité II: La symbolique du mal* (Paris: Seuil); also begins an exhaustive study of Freud
- 1965 – publication of the book, *De l'interprétation. Essai sur Freud*

- 1966-1970 – teaches at the Faculty of Literature at the University of Paris Nanterre
- 1968 – interviews with Gabriel Marcel are published: *Entretiens Paul Ricœur – Gabriel Marcel* (Paris: Aubier)
- 1969 – publishes the first volume of his hermeneutical studies *Le conflit des interprétations: Essais d'herméneutique* (Paris: Seuil)
- 1969-1970 – assumes the post of dean at the University of Paris Nanterre; after a leftist aggression, he resigns as dean and distances himself from intellectual life in France
- 1970 – leaves France and goes to the United States where he assumes the university chair of Paul Tillich at the Chicago University Divinity School, where he teaches until 1990; also teaches at the universities of Louvain, Montreal and Yale, amongst others
- 1973-1987 – teaches again at the University of Paris Nanterre, where in 1987 he becomes professor emeritus
- 1975 – publication of *La métaphore vive* (Paris, Seuil)
- 1983-85 – publication of his trilogy *Temps et récit* (volumes I, II and III, Paris: Seuil)
- 1986 – publication of various books with collected papers *Le Mal. Un défi à la philosophie et à la théologie* (Genève, Labor et Fides), *Du texte à l'action. Essais d'herméneutique II* (Paris, Seuil) and *A l'école de la phénoménologie* (Paris: Vrin)
- 1987 – publication of tribute to Levinas *Répondre d'autrui Emmanuel Lévinas* with papers of Emmanuel Lévinas, Jean-Christophe Aeschlimann and Paul Ricoeur (Paris: la Baconnière)

- 1988 – a conference on Paul Ricoeur is organized by Jean Greisch and Richard Kearney at the International Cultural Center of Cerisy-la-Salle; the proceedings of the conference are published in 1991 under the title *Paul Ricoeur. Les métamorphoses de la raison herméneutique* (Paris: Cerf)
- 1990 – becomes professor emeritus at the University of Chicago; publishes *Soi-même comme un autre* (Paris: Seuil)
- 1991-1994 – his colleted papers on philosophy, politics, and religion are published: *Lectures* (tomes I-III, Paris, Seuil)
- 1995 – publication of *Le Juste* (Paris: Esprit)
- 1997 – publication of *Autrement* (Paris: PUF)
- 2000 – publication of his studies on memory and history – *La Mémoire, l'histoire, l'oubli* (Paris: Seuil)
- 2001 – publication of the second volume of *Le Juste* (Paris: Esprit)
- 2004 – publication of lectures, *Parcours de la reconnaissance*
- 20th May, 2005 – Paul Ricoeur dies at Chatenay Malabry, at 92 years of age

Paul Ricoeur Primary Bibliography:
Books in French and English

Karl Jaspers et la Philosophie de l'existence. (With Michel Dufrenne and a Foreword by Karl Jaspers). Paris: Seuil, 1947.

Gabriel Marcel et Karl Jaspers. Philosophie du mystère et Philosophie du paradoxe. Paris: Temps Présent, 1948.

Le volontaire et l'involontaire (*Philosophie de la volonté*, tome I). Paris: Aubier, 1950; English: *Freedom and Nature: The Voluntary and the Involuntary*. Translated by Erazim V. Kohák. Evanston: Northwestern University Press, 1966.

Husserl Edmund. *Idées directrices pour une phénoménologie.* Translated and introduced by Paul Ricœur. Paris: Gallimard, 1950.

Histoire et vérité. Paris: Seuil, 1955 (second augmented edition 1964; third augmented edition 1967); English: *History and Truth*. Translated by Charles A. Kelbley. Evanston: Northwestern University Press, 1965.

Finitude et Culpabilité, volume I: L'homme faillible (*Philosophie de la volonté*, tome II). Paris: Aubier, 1960; English: *Fallible Man*. Translated by Charles A. Kelbley. Chicago: Henry Regnery, 1965.

Finitude et Culpabilité, volume II: La symbolique du mal (*Philosophie de la volonté*, tome III). Paris: Aubier, 1960; English: *The Symbolism of Evil*. Translated by Emerson Buchanan. New York: Harper and Row, 1967.

De l'interprétation. Essai sur Freud. Paris: Seuil, 1965. English: *Freud and Philosophy: An Essay on Interpretation*. Translated by Denis Savage. New Heaven: Yale University Press, 1970.

Husserl. An Analysis of His Phenomenology. Translated and introduced by Edward G. Ballard and Lester E. Embree. Evanston: Northwestern University Press, 1967.

Entretiens Paul Ricœur – Gabriel Marcel. Paris: Aubier, 1968; English: "Conversations between Paul Ricoeur and Gabriel Marcel," in Gabriel Marcel, *Tragic Wisdom and Beyond*. Translated by Stephen Jolin and Peter McCormick. Evanston, Illinois: Northwestern University Press, 1973.

Le conflit des interprétations. Essais d'herméneutique. Paris: Seuil, 1969; English: *The Conflict of Interpretation. Essays in Hermeneutics*. Edited by Don Ihde, translated by Willis Domingo et al. Evanston: Northwestern University Press, 1974.

The religious significance of atheism (with Alasdair MacIntyre). New York: Columbia University Press, 1969.

Political and Social Essays. Edited by David Stewart and Joseph Bien, translated by Donald Stewart et al. Athens: Ohio University Press, 1974.

La métaphore vive. Paris: Seuil, 1975; English: *The Rule of Metaphor: Multi-Disciplinary Studies in the Creation of Meaning in Language*. Translated by Robert Czerny, Kathleen McLaughlin and John Costello. London: Routledge and Kegan Paul, 1978.

Interpretation Theory: Discourse and the Surplus of Meaning. Fort Worth: The Texas Christian University Press, 1976.

The Contribution of French Historiography to the Theory of History. Oxford: Clarendon Press, 1980.

Temps et récit, tome I: *L'intrigue et le récit philosophique*. Paris: Seuil, 1984; English: *Time and Narrative*, vol. 1. Translated by Kathleen McLaughlin and David Pellauer. Chicago: University of Chicago Press, 1984.

Temps et récit, tome II: *La configuration dans le récit*. Paris: Seuil, 1984; English: *Time and Narrative*, vol. 2. Translated by Kathleen McLaughlin and David Pellauer. Chicago: University of Chicago Press, 1985.

Temps et récit, tome III: *Le temps raconté*. Paris: Seuil, 1985; English: *Time and Narrative*, vol. 3. Translated by Kathleen McLaughlin and David Pellauer. Chicago: University of Chicago Press, 1988

Du texte à l'action. Essais d'herméneutique II. Paris: Seuil, 1986; English: *From Text to Action. Essays in Hermeneutics II*. Translated by Kathleen Blamey and John B. Thompson. London: The Athlone Press, 1991.

A l'école de la phénoménologie. Paris: Vrin, 1986.

Le Mal, Un défi à la Philosophie et à la théologie. Genève: Labor et Fides, 1986; English: *Evil: A Challenge to Philosophy and Theology*. Translated by John Bowden, London/NY: Continuum, 2007.

Répondre d'autrui: Emmanuel Lévinas (With Emmanuel Lévinas and Jean-Christophe Aeschlimann). Paris: la Baconnière, 1987.

Soi-même comme un autre. Paris: Seuil, 1990; English: *Oneself as Another*. Translated by Kathleen Blamey. Chicago: University of Chicago Press, 1992.

Lectures I. Autour du politique. Paris: Seuil, 1991.

Lectures II. La contrée des philosophes. Paris: Seuil, 1992.

Lectures III. Aux frontières de la philosophie. Paris: Seuil, 1994.

Le Juste. Paris: Esprit, 1995; English: *The Just*. Translated by David Pellauer. Chicago: University of Chicago Press, 2000.

Réflexion faite. Autobiographie intellectuelle, Paris: Esprit, 1995; English: "Intellectual Autobiography". In: Lewis E. Hahn (ed.). *The Philosophy of Paul Ricoeur* (The Library of Living Philosophers, Volume XXII). Chicago, La Salle, Illinois: Open Court, 1995.

La critique et la conviction. Entretiens avec François Azouvi et Marc de Launay. Paris: Esprit, 1995; English: *Critique and Conviction*. Translated by Kathleen Blamey. New York: Columbia University Press, 1998.

Tolerance between intolerance and the intolerable. Providence: Berghahn Books, 1996.

Amour et justice. Paris: PUF, 1997.

Autrement. Paris: PUF, 1997.

L'Idéologie et l'utopie. Paris: Seuil, 1997; English: *Lectures on Ideology and Utopia*. Edited, inroduced and translated by George H. Taylor. New York: Columbia University Press, 1986.

Ce qui nous fait penser: la nature et la règle. (With Jean-Pierre Changeux). Paris: Odile Jacob, 1998; English: *What Makes Us Think? A Neuroscientist and a Philosopher Argue about Ethics, Human Nature, and the Brain*. Translated by Malcolm B. DeBevoise. Princeton: Princeton University Press, 2000.

Penser la Bible. (With André LaCocque). Paris: Seuil, 1998; English: *Thinking Biblically: Exegetical and Hermeneutical Studies*. Translated by David Pellauer. Chicago: University of Chicago Press, 1998.

L'unique et le singulier. Entretiens avec Edmond Blattchen. Paris: Alice, 1999.

La Mémoire, l'histoire, l'oubli. Paris: Seuil 2000; English: *Memory, History, Forgetting*. Translated by Kathleen Blamey and David Pellauer. Chicago: University of Chicago Press, 2004.

Le Juste, tome 2. Paris: Esprit 2001; English: *Reflections on the Just*. Translated by David Pellauer. Chicago: University of Chicago Press, 2007.

La lutte pour la reconnaissance et l'économie du don. Paris: Unesco, 2002.

Parcours de la reconnaissance. Trois etudes. Paris: Stock, 2004; English: *The Course of Recognition.* Translated by David Pellauer. Cambridge: Harvard University Press, 2005.

Sur la traduction. Paris: Bayard, 2004; English: *On Translation.* Translated by Eileen Brennan. London and New York: Routledge, 2006.

Vivant jusqu'à la mort suivi de *Fragments.* Paris: Seuil, 2007; English: *Living Up to Death.* Translated by David Pellauer. Chicago: University of Chicago Press, 2009.

**Philosophie, Phänomenologie und Hermeneutik der Werte
Philosophy, Phenomenology and Hermeneutics of Values
Philosophie, Phénoménologie et Herméneutique des Valeurs**
Reihe des Instituts für Axiologische Forschungen

Herausgegeben von Yvanka B. Raynova

Band 1 Simone de Beauvoir. 50 Jahre nach dem *Anderen Geschlecht*. 2. Auflage. Herausgegeben von Yvanka B. Raynova und Susanne Moser. 2004.

Band 2 Yvanka B. Raynova / Susanne Moser (Hrsg.): Das integrale und das gebrochene Ganze. Zum 100. Geburtstag von Leo Gabriel. 2005.

Band 3 Susanne Moser: Freedom and Recognition in the Work of Simone de Beauvoir. 2008.

Band 4 Yvanka B. Raynova: Between the Said and the Unsaid. In Conversation with Paul Ricoeur. Volume I. 2009.

www.peterlang.de